UK 2024 Super Easy Air Fryer Cookbook for Beginn

1800 Days Healthy and Effortless Air Fryer Recipes, Crispy and Nutritious Family Meals | UK Measurements

Marguerite A. Gosnell

Warning-Disclaimer:

The purpose of this book is to educate and entertain. The author or publisher does not guarantee that anyone following the techniques, suggestions, tips, ideas, or strategies will become successful. The author and publisher shall have neither liability or responsibility to anyone with respect to any loss or damage caused, or alleged to be caused, directly or indirectly by the information contained in this book.

CONTENTS

MEASUREMENT CONVERSIONS **10**

Breakfast & Snacks And Fries Recipes **12**

Plantain Fries 12
Blueberry Bread 12
Easy Cheesy Scrambled Eggs 12
Cheese Scones 13
Loaded Hash Browns 13
Raspberry Breakfast Pockets 14
Polenta Fries 14
Potato & Chorizo Frittata 15
Breakfast Sausage Burgers 15
Hard Boiled Eggs Air Fryer Style 15
Egg & Bacon Breakfast Cups 16
French Toast Slices 16
Blanket Breakfast Eggs 17
Breakfast Eggs & Spinach 17
Sweet Potato Fries 17
Bocconcini Balls 18
European Pancakes 18
Cheesy Sausage Breakfast Pockets 18
Oozing Baked Eggs 19
Monte Cristo Breakfast Sandwich 19
Healthy Stuffed Peppers 19
Morning Sausage Wraps 20
Swede Fries 20

Sauces & Snack And Appetiser Recipes **21**

Onion Pakoda 21
Spicy Egg Rolls 21
Korean Chicken Wings 22
Tortellini Bites 22

Cheese Wontons 23
Thai Bites 23
Sweet Potato Crisps 23
Beetroot Crisps 24
Italian Rice Balls 24
Focaccia Bread 25
Popcorn Tofu 25
Peppers With Aioli Dip 26
Lumpia 26
Jalapeño Poppers 27
Mini Aubergine Parmesan Pizza 27
Waffle Fries 27
Pao De Queijo 28
Jalapeño Pockets 28
Salt And Vinegar Chickpeas 29
Tostones 29
Scotch Eggs 29
Mini Calzones 30

Vegetarian & Vegan Recipes 30

Satay Tofu Skewers 30
Roasted Garlic 31
Aubergine Parmigiana 31
Lentil Balls With Zingy Rice 32
Air-fried Artichoke Hearts 32
Veggie Lasagne 33
Gnocchi Caprese 33
Roast Cauliflower & Broccoli 34
Sweet Potato Taquitos 34
Whole Wheat Pizza 35
Goat's Cheese Tartlets 35
Spring Ratatouille 35
Roasted Cauliflower 36
Lentil Burgers 36

Baked Potato 36
Aubergine Dip 37
Sticky Tofu With Cauliflower Rice 37
Spanakopita Bites 38
Falafel Burgers 38
Crispy Potato Peels 39
Broccoli Cheese 39
Arancini 39
Orange Zingy Cauliflower 40
Miso Mushrooms On Sourdough Toast 40
Saganaki 41
Veggie Bakes 41
Artichoke Pasta 41
Spinach And Egg Air Fryer Breakfast Muffins 42
Tomato And Herb Tofu 42
Rainbow Vegetables 43
Butternut Squash Falafel 43
Air Fryer Cheese Sandwich 43
Radish Hash Browns 44
Tempura Veggies 44

Beef & Lamb And Pork Recipes 45

Japanese Pork Chops 45
Steak Dinner 45
Salt And Pepper Belly Pork 46
Sticky Asian Beef 46
Jamaican Jerk Pork 46
Old Fashioned Steak 47
Beef Satay 47
Beef Bulgogi Burgers 48
Traditional Empanadas 48
Steak And Mushrooms 49
Pulled Pork, Bacon, And Cheese Sliders 49
Beef Stirfry 50

Pork Chops With Raspberry And Balsamic 50
Pork With Chinese 5 Spice 51
Hamburgers With Feta 51
Hamburgers 51
Beef And Cheese Empanadas 52
Beef Stuffed Peppers 52
Tahini Beef Bites 53
Butter Steak & Asparagus 53
Sausage Gnocchi One Pot 54
Homemade Crispy Pepperoni Pizza 54
Mustard Pork Tenderloin 55
Cheesy Beef Enchiladas 55
Steak Popcorn Bites 56
Crispy Chili Sausages 56
Pork Taquitos 56
Char Siu Buffalo 57
Copycat Burger 57
Chinese Chilli Beef 58
Asian Meatballs 58
Beef Nacho Pinwheels 58
Cheese & Ham Sliders 59
Beef Stroganoff 59

Fish & Seafood Recipes 60
Thai-style Tuna Fishcakes 60
Salmon Patties 60
Fish In Foil 61
Thai Salmon Patties 61
Air Fried Scallops 61
Coconut Shrimp 62
Thai Fish Cakes 62
Air Fryer Tuna 63
Cajun Prawn Skewers 63
Traditional Fish And Chips 64

Pesto Salmon 64
Garlic Tilapia 65
Maine Seafood 65
Fish Sticks With Tartar Sauce Batter 65
Gluten Free Honey And Garlic Shrimp 66
Salt & Pepper Calamari 66
Crispy Nacho Prawns 66
Cajun Shrimp Boil 67
Ranch Style Fish Fillets 67
Crunchy Fish 67
Store-cupboard Fishcakes 68
Cod Nuggets 68
Garlic-parsley Prawns 68
Peppery Lemon Shrimp 69

Poultry Recipes 69

Chicken And Wheat Stir Fry 69
Hawaiian Chicken 70
Garlic Parmesan Fried Chicken Wings 70
Grain-free Chicken Katsu 71
Air Fried Maple Chicken Thighs 72
Crunchy Chicken Tenders 72
Thai Turkey Burgers 73
Chicken Tikka 73
Pizza Chicken Nuggets 74
Cornflake Chicken Nuggets 74
Chicken Fried Rice 75
Nashville Chicken 75
Chicken And Cheese Chimichangas 76
Chicken Fajitas 76
Chicken Milanese 77
Quick Chicken Nuggets 77
Chicken Jalfrezi 78
Air Fryer Chicken Thigh Schnitzel 78

Whole Chicken 79
Orange Chicken 79
Bbq Chicken Tenders 79
Crispy Cornish Hen 80
Air Fryer Sesame Chicken Thighs 80

Side Dishes Recipes 81

Sweet And Sticky Parsnips And Carrots 81
Ricotta Stuffed Aubergine 81
Garlic And Parsley Potatoes 82
Potato Wedges 82
Crispy Sweet & Spicy Cauliflower 82
Spicy Green Beans 83
Egg Fried Rice 83
Shishito Peppers 83
Mexican Rice 84
Homemade Croquettes 84
Zingy Roasted Carrots 85
Cauliflower With Hot Sauce And Blue Cheese Sauce 85
Celery Root Fries 86
Butternut Squash Fries 86
Sweet Potato Tots 86
Zingy Brussels Sprouts 87
Potato Wedges With Rosemary 87
Butternut Squash 87
Orange Tofu 88
Crispy Cinnamon French Toast 88
Courgette Gratin 89
Corn On The Cob 89
Hasselback New Potatoes 89

Desserts Recipes 90

Chocolate Orange Muffins 90
Mini Egg Buns 90
Shortbread Cookies 91

Strawberry Lemonade Pop Tarts 91
Apple Crumble 92
Thai Fried Bananas 92
Fried Oreos 92
Cinnamon-maple Pineapple Kebabs 93
Baked Nectarines 93
Brazilian Pineapple 93
Peach Pies(2) 94
Chonut Holes 94
Milk And White Chocolate Chip Air Fryer Donuts With Frosting 95
Key Lime Cupcakes 96
Lemon Buns 96
Chocolate Orange Fondant 97
Chocolate Eclairs 97
Banana Maple Flapjack 98
Lemon Pies 98
Strawberry Danish 98
Chocolate Soufflé 99
Cinnamon Biscuit Bites 99
Apple Chips With Yogurt Dip 100
Chocolate Souffle 100
Spiced Apples 100
Peach Pies(1) 101
Breakfast Muffins 101
Pistachio Brownies 102
Banana Bread 102
Chocolate Cake 103
Chocolate Shortbread Balls 103
Sugar Dough Dippers 103
Fruit Scones 104
Grilled Ginger & Coconut Pineapple Rings 104

RECIPES INDEX 105

MEASUREMENT CONVERSIONS

BASIC KITCHEN CONVERSIONS & EQUIVALENTS

DRY MEASUREMENTS CONVERSION CHART

3 TEASPOONS = 1 TABLESPOON = 1/16 CUP
6 TEASPOONS = 2 TABLESPOONS = 1/8 CUP
12 TEASPOONS = 4 TABLESPOONS = 1/4 CUP
24 TEASPOONS = 8 TABLESPOONS = 1/2 CUP
36 TEASPOONS = 12 TABLESPOONS = 3/4 CUP
48 TEASPOONS = 16 TABLESPOONS = 1 CUP

METRIC TO US COOKING CONVER-SIONS

OVEN TEMPERATURES

120 °C = 250 °F
160 °C = 320 °F
180 °C = 350 °F
205 °C = 400 °F
220 °C = 425 °F

LIQUID MEASUREMENTS CONVERSION CHART

8 FLUID OUNCES = 1 CUP = 1/2 PINT = 1/4 QUART
16 FLUID OUNCES = 2 CUPS = 1 PINT = 1/2 QUART
32 FLUID OUNCES = 4 CUPS = 2 PINTS = 1 QUART
1/4 GALLON
128 FLUID OUNCES = 16 CUPS = 8 PINTS = 4 QUARTS = 1 GALLON

BAKING IN GRAMS

1 CUP FLOUR = 140 GRAMS
1 CUP SUGAR = 150 GRAMS
1 CUP POWDERED SUGAR=160 GRAMS
1 CUP HEAVY CREAM = 235 GRAMS

VOLUME

1 MILLILITER=1/5 TEASPOON
5 ML = 1 TEASPOON
15 ML = 1 TABLESPOON
240 ML = 1 CUP OR 8 FLUID OUNCES
1 LITER=34 FL. OUNCES

WEIGHT

1 GRAM = 035 OUNCES
100 GRAMS=3.5 OUNCES
500 GRAMS = 1.1 POUNDS
1 KILOGRAM=35 OUNCES

US TO METRIC COOKING CONVERSIONS

1/5 TSP = 1 ML
1 TSP=5 ML
1 TBSP = 15 ML
1 FL OUNCE = 30 ML
1 CUP=237 ML
1 PINT (2 CUPS) = 473 ML
1 QUART (4 CUPS)=.95 LITER
1GALLON (16 CUPS)=3.8LITERS
1 0Z=28 GRAMS
1 POUND = 454 GRAMS

BUTTER

1 CUP BUTTER=2 STICKS = 8 OUNCES = 230 GRAMS=8 TABLESPOONS

WHAT DOES 1 CUP EQUAL

1 CUP = 8 FLUID OUNCES
1 CUP = 16 TABLESPOONS
1 CUP = 48 TEASPOONS
1 CUP = 1/2 PINT
1 CUP = 1/4 QUART
1 CUP = 1/16 GALLON
1 CUP = 240 ML

BAKING PAN CONVERSIONS

1 CUP ALL-PURPOSE FLOUR=4.5 OZ
1 CUP ROLLED OATS = 3 OZ 1 LARGE EGG = 1.7 OZ
1 CUP BUTTER=80Z 1 CUP MILK = 8 OZ
1 CUP HEAVY CREAM = 8.4 OZ
1 CUP GRANULATED SUGAR=7.1 OZ
1 CUP PACKED BROWN SUGAR = 7.75 OZ
1 CUP VEGETABLE OIL = 7.7 OZ
1 CUP UNSIFTED POWDERED SUGAR = 4.4 OZ

BAKING PAN CONVERSIONS

9-INCH ROUND CAKE PAN= 12 CUPS
10-INCH TUBE PAN =16 CUPS
11-INCH BUNDT PAN = 12 CUPS
9-INCH SPRINGFORM PAN = 10 CUPS
9 X 5 INCH LOAF PAN=8 CUPS
9-INCH SQUARE PAN=8 CUPS

Breakfast & Snacks And Fries Recipes

Plantain Fries

Servings: 2
Cooking Time:xx

Ingredients:

- 1 ripe plantain (yellow and brown outside skin)
- 1 teaspoon olive oil
- ¼ teaspoon salt

Directions:

1. Preheat the air-fryer to 180°C/350°F.
2. Peel the plantain and slice into fries about 6 x 1 cm/2½ x ½ in. Toss the fries in oil and salt, making sure every fry is coated.
3. Tip into the preheated air-fryer in a single layer (you may need to cook them in two batches, depending on the size of your air-fryer) and air-fry for 13–14 minutes until brown on the outside and soft on the inside. Serve immediately.

Blueberry Bread

Servings: 8
Cooking Time:xx

Ingredients:

- 260ml milk
- 3 eggs
- 25g protein powder
- 400g frozen blueberries
- 600g bisquick or pancake mixture

Directions:

1. Take a large mixing bowl and combine all ingredients until smooth
2. Preheat the air fryer to 250°C
3. Place the mixture into a loaf tin
4. Place the tin into the air fryer and cook for 30 minutes
5. A toothpick should come out clean if the bread is cooked

Easy Cheesy Scrambled Eggs

Servings: 1
Cooking Time:xx

Ingredients:

- 1 tbsp butter
- 2 eggs
- 100g grated cheese
- 2 tbsp milk
- Salt and pepper for seasoning

Directions:

1. Add the butter inside the air fryer pan and cook at 220°C until the butter has melted
2. Add the eggs and milk to a bowl and combine, seasoning to your liking
3. Pour the eggs into the butter panned cook for 3 minutes, stirring around lightly to scramble
4. Add the cheese and cook for another 2 more minutes

Cheese Scones

Servings:12
Cooking Time:xx
Ingredients:

- ½ teaspoon baking powder
- 210 g/1½ cups self-raising/self-rising flour (gluten-free if you wish), plus extra for dusting
- 50 g/3½ tablespoons cold butter, cubed
- 125 g/1½ cups grated mature Cheddar
- a pinch of cayenne pepper
- a pinch of salt
- 100 ml/7 tablespoons milk, plus extra for brushing the tops of the scones

Directions:

1. Mix the baking powder with the flour in a bowl, then add the butter and rub into the flour to form a crumblike texture. Add the cheese, cayenne pepper and salt and stir. Then add the milk, a little at a time, and bring together into a ball of dough.
2. Dust your work surface with flour. Roll the dough flat until about 1.5 cm/⅝ in. thick. Cut out the scones using a 6-cm/2½-in. diameter cookie cutter. Gather the offcuts into a ball, re-roll and cut more scones – you should get about 12 scones from the mixture. Place the scones on an air-fryer liner or a piece of pierced parchment paper.
3. Preheat the air-fryer to 180°C/350°F.
4. Add the scones to the preheated air-fryer and air-fry for 8 minutes, turning them over halfway to cook the other side. Remove and allow to cool a little, then serve warm.

Loaded Hash Browns

Servings: 4
Cooking Time:xx
Ingredients:

- 4 large potatoes
- 2 tbsp bicarbonate of soda
- 1 tbsp salt
- 1 tbsp black pepper
- 1 tsp cayenne pepper
- 2 tbsp olive oil
- 1 large chopped onion
- 1 chopped red pepper
- 1 chopped green pepper

Directions:

1. Grate the potatoes
2. Squeeze out any water contained within the potatoes
3. Take a large bowl of water and add the potatoes
4. Add the bicarbonate of soda, combine everything and leave to soak for 25 minutes
5. Drain the water away and carefully pat the potatoes to dry
6. Transfer your potatoes into another bowl
7. Add the spices and oil
8. Combining everything well, tossing to coat evenly
9. Place your potatoes into your fryer basket
10. Set to 200°C and cook for 10 minutes
11. Give the potatoes a shake and add the peppers and the onions
12. Cook for another 10 minutes

Raspberry Breakfast Pockets

Servings: 1

Cooking Time:xx

Ingredients:

- 2 slices of sandwich bread
- 1 tbsp soft cream cheese
- 1 tbsp raspberry jam
- 1 tbsp milk
- 1 egg

Directions:

1. Take one slice of the bread and add one tablespoon of jam into the middle
2. Take the second slice and add the cream cheese into the middle
3. Using a blunt knife, spread the jam and the cheese across the bread, but don't go to the outer edges
4. Take a small bowl and whisk the eggs and the milk together
5. Set your fryer to 190°C and spray with a little oil
6. Dip your sandwich into the egg and arrange inside your fryer
7. Cook for 5 minutes on the first side, turn and cook for another 2 minutes

Polenta Fries

Servings: 6

Cooking Time:xx

Ingredients:

- 800 ml/scant 3½ cups water
- 1½ vegetable stock cubes
- ¾ teaspoon dried oregano
- ¾ teaspoon freshly ground black pepper
- 200 g/1⅓ cups quick-cook polenta/cornmeal
- 2 teaspoons olive oil
- 55 g/6 tablespoons plain/all-purpose flour (gluten-free if you wish)
- garlic mayonnaise, to serve

Directions:

1. Bring the water and stock cubes to the boil in a saucepan with the oregano and black pepper. Stir in the polenta/cornmeal and continue to stir until the mixture becomes significantly more solid and is hard to stir – this should take about 5–6 minutes.
2. Grease a 15 x 15-cm/6 x 6-in. baking pan with some of the olive oil. Tip the polenta into the baking pan, smoothing down with the back of a wet spoon. Leave to cool at room temperature for about 30 minutes, then pop into the fridge for at least an hour.
3. Remove the polenta from the fridge and carefully tip out onto a chopping board. Slice the polenta into fingers 7.5 x 1 x 2 cm/3 x ½ x ¾ in. Roll the polenta fingers in the flour, then spray or drizzle the remaining olive oil over the fingers.
4. Preheat the air-fryer to 200°C/400°F.
5. Lay the fingers apart from one another in a single layer in the preheated air-fryer (you may need to cook these in batches, depending on the size of your air-fryer). Air-fry for 9 minutes, turning once halfway through cooking. Serve immediately with garlic mayonnaise.

Potato & Chorizo Frittata

Servings: 2
Cooking Time:xx
Ingredients:

- 3 eggs
- 1 sliced chorizo sausage
- 1 potato, boiled and cubed
- 50g feta cheese
- 50g frozen sweetcorn
- A pinch of salt
- 1 tbsp olive oil

Directions:

1. Add a little olive oil to the frying basket
2. Add the corn, potato, and sliced chorizo to the basket
3. Cook at 180°C until the sausage is a little brown
4. In a small bowl, beat together the eggs with a little seasoning
5. Pour the eggs into the pan
6. Crumble the feta on top
7. Cook for 5 minutes
8. Remove and serve in slices

Breakfast Sausage Burgers

Servings: 2
Cooking Time:xx
Ingredients:

- 8 links of your favourite sausage
- Salt and pepper to taste

Directions:

1. Remove the sausage from the skins and use a fork to create a smooth mixture
2. Season to your liking
3. Shape the sausage mixture into burgers or patties
4. Preheat your air fryer to 260°C
5. Arrange the burgers in the fryer, so they are not touching each other
6. Cook for 8 minutes
7. Serve still warm

Hard Boiled Eggs Air Fryer Style

Servings: 2
Cooking Time:xx
Ingredients:

- 4 large eggs
- 1 tsp cayenne pepper
- Salt and pepper for seasoning

Directions:

1. Preheat the air fryer to 220°C
2. Take a wire rack and place inside the air fryer
3. Lay the eggs on the rack
4. Cook for between 15-17 minutes, depending upon how you like your eggs
5. Remove from the fryer and place in a bowl of cold water for around 5 minutes
6. Peel and season with the cayenne and the salt and pepper

Egg & Bacon Breakfast Cups

Servings: 8
Cooking Time:xx

Ingredients:

- 6 eggs
- 1 chopped red pepper
- 1 chopped green pepper
- 1 chopped yellow pepper
- 2 tbsp double cream
- 50g chopped spinach
- 50g grated cheddar cheese
- 50g grated mozzarella cheese
- 3 slices of cooked bacon, crumbled into pieces

Directions:

1. Take a large mixing bowl and crack the eggs
2. Add the cream and season with a little salt and pepper, combining everything well
3. Add the peppers, spinach, onions, both cheeses, and the crumbled bacon, combining everything once more
4. You will need silicone moulds or cups for this part, and you should pour equal amounts of the mixture into 8 cups
5. Cook at 150°C for around 12 or 15 minutes, until the eggs are cooked properly

French Toast Slices

Servings: 1
Cooking Time:xx

Ingredients:

- 2 eggs
- 5 slices sandwich bread
- 100ml milk
- 2 tbsp flour
- 3 tbsp sugar
- 1 tsp ground cinnamon
- 1/2 tsp vanilla extract
- Pinch of salt

Directions:

1. Preheat your air fryer to 220°C
2. Take your bread and cut it into three pieces of the same size
3. Take a mixing bowl and combine the other ingredients until smooth
4. Dip the bread into the mixture, coating evenly
5. Take a piece of parchment paper and lay it inside the air fryer
6. Arrange the bread on the parchment paper in one layer
7. Cook for 5 minutes
8. Turn and cook for another 5 minutes

Blanket Breakfast Eggs

Servings: 2
Cooking Time:xx

Ingredients:

- 2 eggs
- 2 slices of sandwich bread
- Olive oil spray
- Salt and pepper to taste

Directions:

1. Preheat your air fryer to 190°C and spray with a little oil
2. Meanwhile, take your bread and cut a hole into the middle of each piece
3. Place one slice inside your fryer and crack one egg into the middle
4. Season with a little salt and pepper
5. Cook for 5 minutes, before turning over and cooking for a further 2 minutes
6. Remove the first slice and repeat the process with the remaining slice of bread and egg

Breakfast Eggs & Spinach

Servings: 4
Cooking Time:xx

Ingredients:

- 500g wilted, fresh spinach
- 200g sliced deli ham
- 1 tbsp olive oil
- 4 eggs
- 4 tsp milk
- Salt and pepper to taste
- 1 tbsp butter for cooking

Directions:

1. Preheat your air fryer to 180°C
2. You will need 4 small ramekin dishes, coated with a little butter
3. Arrange the wilted spinach, ham, 1 teaspoon of milk and 1 egg into each ramekin and season with a little salt and pepper
4. Place in the fryer 15 to 20 minutes, until the egg is cooked to your liking
5. Allow to cool before serving

Sweet Potato Fries

Servings: 4
Cooking Time:xx

Ingredients:

- 2 medium sweet potatoes
- 2 teaspoons olive oil
- ½ teaspoon salt
- ½ teaspoon chilli/hot red pepper flakes
- ½ teaspoon smoked paprika

Directions:

1. Preheat the air-fryer to 190°C/375°F.
2. Peel the sweet potatoes and slice into fries about 1 x 1 cm/½ x ½ in. by the length of the potato. Toss the sweet potato fries in the oil, salt, chilli and paprika, making sure every fry is coated.
3. Tip into the preheated air-fryer in a single layer (you may need to cook them in two batches, depending on the size of your air-fryer). Air-fry for 10 minutes, turning once halfway during cooking. Serve immediately.

Bocconcini Balls

Servings: 2

Cooking Time:xx

Ingredients:

- 70 g/½ cup plus ½ tablespoon plain/all-purpose flour (gluten-free if you wish)
- 1 egg, beaten
- 70 g/1 cup dried breadcrumbs (gluten-free if you wish; see page 9)
- 10 bocconcini

Directions:

1. Preheat the air-fryer to 200°C/400°F.
2. Place the flour, egg and breadcrumbs on 3 separate plates. Dip each bocconcini ball first in the flour to coat, then the egg, shaking off any excess before rolling in the breadcrumbs.
3. Add the breaded bocconcini to the preheated air-fryer and air-fry for 5 minutes (no need to turn them during cooking). Serve immediately.

European Pancakes

Servings: 5

Cooking Time:xx

Ingredients:

- 3 large eggs
- 130g flour
- 140ml whole milk
- 2 tbsp unsweetened apple sauce
- A pinch of salt

Directions:

1. Set your fryer to 200°C and add five ramekins inside to heat up
2. Place all your ingredients inside a blender to combine
3. Spray the ramekins with a little cooking spray
4. Pour the batter into the ramekins carefully
5. Fry for between 6-8 minutes, depending on your preference
6. Serve with your favourite toppings

Cheesy Sausage Breakfast Pockets

Servings: 2

Cooking Time:xx

Ingredients:

- 1 packet of regular puff pastry
- 4 sausages, cooked and crumbled into pieces
- 5 eggs
- 50g cooked bacon
- 50g grated cheddar cheese

Directions:

1. Scramble your eggs in your usual way
2. Add the sausage and the bacon as you are cooking the eggs and combine well
3. Take your pastry sheets and cut rectangular shapes
4. Add a little of the egg and meat mixture to one half of each pastry piece
5. Fold the rectangles over and use a fork to seal down the edges
6. Place your pockets into your air fryer and cook at 190°C for 10 minutes
7. Allow to cool before serving

Oozing Baked Eggs

Servings: 2
Cooking Time:xx

Ingredients:

- 4 eggs
- 140g smoked gouda cheese, cut into small pieces
- Salt and pepper to taste

Directions:

1. You will need two ramekin dishes and spray each one before using
2. Crack two eggs into each ramekin dish
3. Add half of the Gouda cheese to each dish
4. Season and place into the air fryer
5. Cook at 350°C for 15 minutes, until the eggs are cooked as you like them

Monte Cristo Breakfast Sandwich

Servings: 4
Cooking Time:xx

Ingredients:

- 1 egg
- 2 slices of sandwich bread
- 1/4 tsp vanilla extract
- 4 slices of sliced Swiss cheese
- 4 slices of sliced deli ham
- 4 slices of sliced turkey
- 1 tsp melted butter
- Powdered sugar for serving

Directions:

1. In a small bowl, mix together the egg and vanilla extract, combining well
2. Take your bread and assemble your sandwich, starting with a slice of cheese, then the ham, turkey, and then another slice of the cheese, with the other slice of bread on the top
3. Compress the sandwich a little, so it cooks better
4. Take a piece of cooking foil and brush over it with the butter
5. Take your sandwich and dip each side into the egg mixture, leaving it to one side for around half a minute
6. Place the sandwich on the foil and place it inside your fryer
7. Cook at 200°C for around 10 minutes, before turning the sandwich over and cooking for another 8 minutes
8. Transfer your sandwich onto a plate and sprinkle with a little powdered sugar

Healthy Stuffed Peppers

Servings: 2
Cooking Time:xx

Ingredients:

- 1 large bell pepper, deseeded and cut into halves
- 1 tsp olive oil
- 4 large eggs
- Salt and pepper to taste

Directions:

1. Take your peppers and rub a little olive oil on the edges
2. Into each pepper, crack one egg and season with salt and pepper
3. You will need to insert a trivet into your air fryer to hold the peppers, and then arrange the peppers evenly
4. Set your fryer to 200°C and cook for 13 minutes
5. Once cooked, remove and serve with a little more seasoning, if required

Morning Sausage Wraps

Servings: 8
Cooking Time:xx

Ingredients:

- 8 sausages, chopped into pieces
- 2 slices of cheddar cheese, cut into quarters
- 1 can of regular crescent roll dough
- 8 wooden skewers

Directions:

1. Take the dough and separate each one
2. Cut open the sausages evenly
3. The one of your crescent rolls and on the widest part, add a little sausage and then a little cheese
4. Roll the dough and tuck it until you form a triangle
5. Repeat this for four times and add into your air fryer
6. Cook at 190°C for 3 minutes
7. Remove your dough and add a skewer for serving
8. Repeat with the other four pieces of dough

Swede Fries

Servings: 4
Cooking Time:xx

Ingredients:

- 1 medium swede/rutabaga
- ½ teaspoon salt
- ½ teaspoon freshly ground black pepper
- 1½ teaspoons dried thyme
- 1 tablespoon olive oil

Directions:

1. Preheat the air-fryer to 160°C/325°F.
2. Peel the swede/rutabaga and slice into fries about 6 x 1 cm/2½ x ½ in., then toss the fries in the salt, pepper, thyme and oil, making sure every fry is coated.
3. Tip into the preheated air-fryer in a single layer (you may need to cook them in two batches, depending on the size of your air-fryer) and air-fry for 15 minutes, shaking the drawer halfway through. Then increase the temperature to 180°C/350°F and cook for a further 5 minutes. Serve immediately.

Onion Pakoda

Servings: 2
Cooking Time:xx

Ingredients:

- 200g gram flour
- 2 onions, thinly sliced
- 1 tbsp crushed coriander seeds
- 1 tsp chilli powder
- ¾ tsp salt
- ¼ tsp turmeric
- ¼ tsp baking soda

Directions:

1. Mix all the ingredients together in a large bowl
2. Make bite sized pakodas
3. Heat the air fryer to 200°C
4. Line the air fryer with foil
5. Place the pakoda in the air fryer and cook for 5 minutes
6. Turn over and cook for a further 5 minutes

Spicy Egg Rolls

Servings: 4
Cooking Time:xx

Ingredients:

- 1 rotisserie chicken, shredded and diced
- 3 tbsp water
- 3 tbsp taco seasoning
- 1 can of black beans, drained
- 1 red bell pepper, diced
- 1 can of sweetcorn, drained
- 1 jalapeño pepper, deseeded and minced
- 2 packs of egg roll wrappers
- 250g grated strong cheddar cheese
- 250g grated Monterey Jack cheese

Directions:

1. Take a medium bowl and add the water and taco seasoning, combining well
2. Add the shredded check and coat well
3. Lay out an egg roll wrapper and arrange it so that one corner is facing towards you
4. Add 3 tablespoons of the mixture into the wrapper, just below the middle
5. Roll the corner facing you upwards, pulling it tightly closed over the mixture
6. Add a little water to the other two corners and fold into the centre and pat down to seal
7. Roll the rest of the wrapper up, so that all the corners are sealed
8. Repeat with the rest of the mixture
9. Preheat the air fryer to 220°C
10. Cook for 9 minutes and turn over at the halfway point

Korean Chicken Wings

Servings: 2
Cooking Time:xx

Ingredients:

- 25ml soy sauce
- 40g brown sugar
- 2 tbsp hot pepper paste
- 1 tsp sesame oil
- ½ tsp ginger paste
- ½ tsp garlic paste
- 2 green onions, chopped
- 400g chicken wings
- 1 tbsp vegetable oil

Directions:

1. Preheat air fryer to 200°C
2. Place all ingredients apart from chicken wings and vegetable oil in a pan and simmer for about 4 minutes set aside
3. Massage the vegetable oil into the chicken wings
4. Place in the air fryer and cook for about 10 minutes
5. Turn and cook for a further 10 minutes
6. Coat the wings in the sauce and return to the air fryer
7. Cook for about 2 minutes

Tortellini Bites

Servings: 6
Cooking Time:xx

Ingredients:

- 200g cheese tortellini
- 150g flour
- 100g panko bread crumbs
- 50g grated parmesan
- 1 tsp dried oregano
- 2 eggs
- ½ tsp garlic powder
- ½ tsp chilli flakes
- Salt
- Pepper

Directions:

1. Cook the tortellini according to the packet instructions
2. Mix the panko, parmesan, oregano, garlic powder, chilli flakes salt and pepper in a bowl
3. Beat the eggs in another bowl and place the flour in a third bowl
4. Coat the tortellini in flour, then egg and then in the panko mix
5. Place in the air fryer and cook at 185°C for 10 minutes until crispy
6. Serve with marinara sauce for dipping

Cheese Wontons

Servings: 8
Cooking Time:xx

Ingredients:

- 8 wonton wrappers
- 1 carton pimento cheese
- Small dish of water
- Cooking spray

Directions:

1. Place one tsp of cheese in the middle of each wonton wrapper
2. Brush the edges of each wonton wrapper with water
3. Fold over to create a triangle and seal
4. Heat the air fryer to 190°C
5. Spray the wontons with cooking spray
6. Place in the air fryer and cook for 3 minutes
7. Turnover and cook for a further 3 minutes

Thai Bites

Servings: 4
Cooking Time:xx

Ingredients:

- 400g pork mince
- 1 onion
- 1 tsp garlic paste
- 1 tbsp soy
- 1 tbsp Worcester sauce
- Salt and pepper
- 2 tsp Thai curry paste
- ½ lime juice and zest
- 1 tsp mixed spice
- 1 tsp Chinese spice
- 1 tsp coriander

Directions:

1. Place all ingredients in a bowl and mix well
2. Shape into balls
3. Place in the air fryer and cook at 180°C for 15 minutes

Sweet Potato Crisps

Servings: 4
Cooking Time:xx

Ingredients:

- 1 sweet potato, peeled and thinly sliced
- 2 tbsp oil
- ¼ tsp salt
- ¼ tsp pepper
- 1 tsp chopped rosemary
- Cooking spray

Directions:

1. Place all ingredients in a bowl and mix well
2. Place in the air fryer and cook at 175°C for about 15 minutes until crispy

Beetroot Crisps

Servings: 2
Cooking Time:xx

Ingredients:

- 3 medium beetroots
- 2 tbsp oil
- Salt to taste

Directions:

1. Peel and thinly slice the beetroot
2. Coat with the oil and season with salt
3. Preheat the air fryer to 200°C
4. Place in the air fryer and cook for 12-18 minutes until crispy

Italian Rice Balls

Servings: 2
Cooking Time:xx

Ingredients:

- 400g cooked rice
- 25g breadcrumbs, plus an extra 200g for breading
- 2 tbsp flour, plus an extra 2 tbsp for breading
- 1 tbsp cornstarch, plus an extra 3 tbsp for breading
- 1 chopped bell pepper
- 1 chopped onion
- 2 tbsp olive oil
- 1 tsp red chilli flakes
- 5 chopped mozzarella cheese sticks
- A little water for the breading
- Salt and pepper for seasoning

Directions:

1. Place the cooked rice into a bowl and mash with a fork. Place to one side
2. Take a saucepan and add the oil, salting the onion and peppers until they're both soft
3. Add the chilli flakes and a little salt and combine
4. Add the mixture to the mashed rice and combine
5. Add the 2 tbsp flour and 1 tbsp cornstarch, along with the 25g breadcrumbs and combine well
6. Use your hands to create balls with the mixture
7. Stuff a piece of the mozzarella inside the balls and form around it
8. Take a bowl and add the rest of the flour, corn starch and a little seasoning, with a small amount of water to create a thick batter
9. Take another bowl and add the rest of the breadcrumbs
10. Dip each rice ball into the batter and then the breadcrumbs
11. Preheat the air fryer to 220°C
12. Cook for 6 minutes, before shaking and cooking for another 6 minutes

Focaccia Bread

Servings: 8
Cooking Time:xx

Ingredients:

- 500g pizza dough
- 3 tbsp olive oil
- 2-3 garlic cloves, chopped
- ¼ tsp red pepper flakes
- 50g parsley
- 1 tsp basil
- 100g chopped red peppers
- 60g black olives halved
- 60g green olives halved
- Salt and pepper to taste

Directions:

1. Preheat the air fryer to 180°C, make indentations in the pizza dough with your finger tips and set aside
2. Heat the olive oil in a pan add the garlic and cook for a few minutes, add the remaining ingredients and cook for another 5-8 minutes not letting the oil get too hot
3. Spread the oil mix over the dough with a spatula
4. Place in the air fryer and cook for 12-15 minutes

Popcorn Tofu

Servings: 4
Cooking Time:xx

Ingredients:

- 400g firm tofu
- 100g chickpea flour
- 100g oatmeal
- 2 tbsp yeast
- 150ml milk
- 400g breadcrumbs
- 1 tsp garlic powder
- 1 tsp onion powder
- 1 tbsp dijon mustard
- ½ tsp salt
- ½ tsp pepper
- 2 tbsp vegetable bouillon

Directions:

1. Rip the tofu into pieces. Place the breadcrumbs into a bowl, in another bowl mix the remaining ingredients
2. Dip the tofu into the batter mix and then dip into the breadcrumbs
3. Heat the air fryer to 175°C
4. Place the tofu in the air fryer and cook for 12 minutes shaking halfway through

Peppers With Aioli Dip

Servings: 4
Cooking Time:xx

Ingredients:

- 250g shishito peppers
- 2 tsp avocado oil
- 5 tbsp mayonnaise
- 2 tbsp lemon juice
- 1 minced clove of garlic
- 1 tbsp chopped parsley
- Salt and pepper for seasoning

Directions:

1. Take a medium bowl and combine the mayonnaise with the lemon juice, garlic, parsley and seasoning and create a smooth dip
2. Preheat the air fryer to 220°C
3. Toss the peppers in the oil and add to the air fryer
4. Cook for 4 minutes, until the peppers are soft and blistered on the outside
5. Remove and serve with the dip

Lumpia

Servings: 16
Cooking Time:xx

Ingredients:

- 400g Italian sausage
- 1 sliced onion
- 1 chopped carrot
- 50g chopped water chestnuts
- Cooking spray
- 2 cloves minced, garlic
- 2 tbsp soy sauce
- ½ tsp salt
- ¼ tsp ground ginger
- 16 spring roll wrappers

Directions:

1. Cook sausage in a pan for about 5 minutes. Add green onions, onions, water chestnuts and carrot cook for 7 minutes
2. Add garlic and cook for a further 2 minutes
3. Add the soy sauce, salt and ginger, stir to mix well
4. Add filling to each spring roll wrapper.
5. Roll over the bottom and tuck in the sides, continue to roll up the spring roll
6. Spray with cooking spray and place in the air fryer
7. Cook at 200°C for 4 minutes turn and cook for a further 4 minutes

Jalapeño Poppers

Servings: 2
Cooking Time:xx

Ingredients:

- 10 jalapeños, halved and deseeded
- 100g cream cheese
- 50g parsley
- 150g breadcrumbs

Directions:

1. Mix 1/2 the breadcrumbs with the cream cheese
2. Add the parsley
3. Stuff the peppers with the cream cheese mix
4. Top the peppers with the remaining breadcrumbs
5. Heat the air fryer to 185°C
6. Place in the air fryer and cook for 6-8 minutes

Mini Aubergine Parmesan Pizza

Servings: 8
Cooking Time:xx

Ingredients:

- 1 aubergine, cut into ½ inch slices
- Salt to taste
- 1 egg
- 1 tbsp water
- 100g bread crumbs
- 75g grated parmesan
- 6 tbsp pizza sauce
- 50g sliced olives
- 75g grated mozzarella
- Basil to garnish

Directions:

1. Preheat air fryer to 160°C
2. Mix egg and water together and in another bowl mix the breadcrumbs and parmesan
3. Dip the aubergine in the egg then coat with the breadcrumbs
4. Place in the air fryer and cook for 10 minutes
5. Spoon pizza sauce on the aubergine, add olives and sprinkle with mozzarella
6. Cook for about 4 minutes until cheese has melted

Waffle Fries

Servings: 4
Cooking Time:xx

Ingredients:

- 2 large potatoes, russet potatoes work best
- 1 tsp salt for seasoning
- Waffle cutter

Directions:

1. Peel the potatoes and slice using the waffle cutter. You can also use a mandolin cutter that has a blade
2. Transfer the potatoes to a bowl and season with the salt, coating evenly
3. Add to the air fryer and cook at 220°C for 15 minutes, shaking every so often

Pao De Queijo

Servings: 20
Cooking Time:xx
Ingredients:

- 150g sweet starch
- 150g sour starch
- 50ml milk
- 25ml water
- 25ml olive oil
- 1 tsp salt
- 2 eggs
- 100g grated cheese
- 50g grated parmesan

Directions:

1. Preheat the air fryer to 170°C
2. Mix the starch together in a bowl until well mixed
3. Add olive oil, milk and water to a pan, bring to the boil and reduce the heat
4. Add the starch and mix until all the liquid is absorbed
5. Add the eggs and mix to a dough
6. Add the cheeses and mix well
7. Form the dough into balls
8. Line the air fryer with parchment paper
9. Bake in the air fryer for 8-10 minutes

Jalapeño Pockets

Servings: 4
Cooking Time:xx
Ingredients:

- 1 chopped onion
- 60g cream cheese
- 1 jalapeño, chopped
- 8 wonton wrappers
- ¼ tsp garlic powder
- ⅛ tsp onion powder

Directions:

1. Cook the onion in a pan for 5 minutes until softened
2. Add to a bowl and mix with the remaining ingredients
3. Lay the wonton wrappers out and add filling to each one
4. Fold over to create a triangle and seal with water around the edges
5. Heat the air fryer to 200°C
6. Place in the air fryer and cook for about 4 minutes

Salt And Vinegar Chickpeas

Servings: 5
Cooking Time:xx

Ingredients:

- 1 can chickpeas
- 100ml white vinegar
- 1 tbsp olive oil
- Salt to taste

Directions:

1. Combine chickpeas and vinegar in a pan, simmer remove from heat and stand for 30 minutes
2. Preheat the air fryer to 190°C
3. Drain chickpeas
4. Place chickpeas in the air fryer and cook for about 4 minutes
5. Pour chickpeas into an ovenproof bowl drizzle with oil, sprinkle with salt
6. Place bowl in the air fryer and cook for another 4 minutes

Tostones

Servings: 4
Cooking Time:xx

Ingredients:

- 2 unripe plantains
- Olive oil cooking spray
- 300ml of water
- Salt to taste

Directions:

1. Preheat the air fryer to 200°C
2. Slice the tips off the plantain
3. Cut the plantain into 1 inch chunks
4. Place in the air fryer spray with oil and cook for 5 minutes
5. Remove the plantain from the air fryer and smash to ½ inch pieces
6. Soak in a bowl of salted water
7. Remove from the water and return to the air fryer season with salt cook for 5 minutes
8. Turn and cook for another 5 minutes

Scotch Eggs

Servings: 6
Cooking Time:xx

Ingredients:

- 300g pork sausage
- 6 hard boiled eggs, shelled
- 50g cup flour
- 2 eggs, beaten
- 1 cup breadcrumbs
- Cooking spray

Directions:

1. Divide sausage into 6 portions
2. Place an egg in the middle of each portion and wrap around the egg
3. Dip the sausage in flour, then egg and then coat in breadcrumbs
4. Place in the air fryer and cook at 200°C for 12 minutes

Mini Calzones

Servings: 16

Cooking Time:xx

Ingredients:

- Flour for rolling out the dough
- 1 round pizza dough
- 100g pizza sauce

Directions:

1. Roll out the dough to ¼ inch thick
2. Cut out 8-10 dough rounds using a cutter
3. Re-roll the dough and cut out another 6 rounds
4. Top each round with pizza sauce, cheese and pepperoni
5. Fold dough over and pinch the edges to seal
6. Heat the air fryer to 190°C
7. Place the calzone in the air fryer and cook for about 8 minutes until golden brown

Vegetarian & Vegan Recipes

Satay Tofu Skewers

Servings: 2

Cooking Time:xx

Ingredients:

- 300 g/10½ oz. firm tofu
- Lime-Almond Satay Sauce (see page 87), to serve
- MARINADE
- 200 ml/¾ cup coconut milk (including the thick part from the can)
- 1 plump garlic clove, finely chopped
- 2 teaspoons grated ginger
- 2 tablespoons soy sauce
- 1 heaped tablespoon smooth peanut butter
- 1 tablespoon maple syrup
- 1 tablespoon mild curry powder
- 1 tablespoon fish sauce or plant-based alternative

Directions:

1. Cut the tofu into 2 x 2-cm/¾ x ¾-in. cubes. Mix the marinade ingredients thoroughly, then toss in the tofu cubes. Once the tofu cubes are covered in the marinade, leave in the fridge to marinate for at least 4 hours.
2. Preheat the air-fryer to 180°C/350°F.
3. Thread the tofu cubes onto 4 skewers that fit inside your air-fryer. Place on an air-fryer liner or a piece of pierced parchment paper and add to the preheated air-fryer. Air-fry for 12 minutes, turning over once during cooking.
4. Serve the tofu skewers alongside a bowl of the Lime-Almond Satay Sauce.

Roasted Garlic

Servings: 2
Cooking Time:xx

Ingredients:

- 1 head of garlic
- Drizzle of olive oil
- Salt and pepper for seasoning

Directions:

1. Remove paper peel from garlic
2. Place in foil and drizzle with oil
3. Place in the air fryer and cook at 200°C for 20 minutes
4. Season before serving

Aubergine Parmigiana

Servings: 2 As A Main Or 4 As A Side
Cooking Time:xx

Ingredients:

- 2 small or 1 large aubergine/eggplant, sliced 5 mm/¼ in. thick
- 1 tablespoon olive oil
- ¾ teaspoon salt
- 200 g/7 oz. mozzarella, sliced
- ½ teaspoon freshly ground black pepper
- 20 g/¼ cup finely grated Parmesan
- green vegetables, to serve
- SAUCE
- 135 g/5 oz. passata/strained tomatoes
- 1 teaspoon dried oregano
- ¼ teaspoon garlic salt
- 1 tablespoon olive oil

Directions:

1. Preheat the air-fryer to 200°C/400°F.
2. Rub each of the aubergine/eggplant slices with olive oil and salt. Divide the slices into two batches. Place one batch of the aubergine slices in the preheated air-fryer and air-fry for 4 minutes on one side, then turn over and air-fry for 2 minutes on the other side. Lay these on the base of a gratin dish that fits into your air-fryer.
3. Air-fry the second batch of aubergine slices in the same way. Whilst they're cooking, mix together the sauce ingredients in a small bowl.
4. Spread the sauce over the aubergines in the gratin dish. Add a layer of the mozzarella slices, then season with pepper. Add a second layer of aubergine slices, then top with Parmesan.
5. Place the gratin dish in the air-fryer and air-fry for 6 minutes, until the mozzarella is melted and the top of the dish is golden brown. Serve immediately with green vegetables on the side.

Lentil Balls With Zingy Rice

Servings: 4
Cooking Time:xx

Ingredients:

- 2 cans lentils
- 200g walnut halves
- 3 tbsp dried mushrooms
- 3 tbsp parsley
- 1 ½ tbsp tomato paste
- ¾ tsp salt
- ½ tsp pepper
- 100g bread crumbs
- 400ml water
- 200g rice
- 2 tbsp lemon juice
- 2 tsp lemon zest
- Salt to taste

Directions:

1. Preheat air fryer to 190°C
2. Place the lentils, walnuts, mushrooms, parsley, tomato paste, salt, pepper in a food processor and blend
3. Fold in the bread crumbs
4. Form the mix into balls and place in the air fryer
5. Cook for 10 minutes turn then cook for a further 5 minutes
6. Add the rice to a pan with water, bring to the boil and simmer for 20 minutes
7. Stir in the lemon juice, lemon zest and salt. Serve

Air-fried Artichoke Hearts

Servings: 7
Cooking Time:xx

Ingredients:

- 14 artichoke hearts
- 200g flour
- ¼ tsp baking powder
- Salt
- 6 tbsp water
- 6 tbsp breadcrumbs
- ¼ tsp basil
- ¼ tsp oregano
- ¼ tsp garlic powder
- ¼ tsp paprika

Directions:

1. Mix the baking powder, salt, flour and water in a bowl
2. In another bowl combine the breadcrumbs and seasonings
3. Dip the artichoke in the batter then coat in breadcrumbs
4. Place in the air fryer and cook at 180°C for 8 minutes

Veggie Lasagne

Servings: 1
Cooking Time:xx

Ingredients:

- 2 lasagne sheets
- Pinch of salt
- 100g pasta sauce
- 50g ricotta
- 60g chopped basil
- 40g chopped spinach
- 3 tbsp grated courgette

Directions:

1. Break the lasagne sheets in half, bring a pan of water to boil
2. Cook the lasagne sheets for about 8 minutes, drain and pat dry
3. Add 2 tbsp of pasta sauce to a mini loaf tin
4. Add a lasagne sheet, top with ricotta, basil and spinach, then add courgette
5. Place another lasagne sheet on top
6. Add a couple of tbsp pasta sauce, basil, spinach and courgette
7. Add the last lasagne sheet, top with pasta sauce and ricotta
8. Cover with foil and place in the air fryer
9. Cook at 180°C for 10 mins, remove foil and cook for another 3 minutes

Gnocchi Caprese

Servings: 2
Cooking Time:xx

Ingredients:

- 1 packet of gnocchi
- 150g cherry tomatoes, cut into halves
- 2 tbsp olive oil
- 2 tbsp balsamic vinegar
- 3 pressed cloves of garlic
- 200g basil, chopped
- 200g mini mozzarella balls
- 150g grated Parmesan
- Salt and pepper for seasoning

Directions:

1. Preheat the air fryer to 220°C
2. Take a large bowl and add the cherry tomatoes, gnocchi, oil, balsamic vinegar, garlic and seasoning, making sure that everything is well coated
3. Transfer to the air fryer basket
4. Cook for 10 minutes, shaking the basket every few minutes
5. Once cooked, transfer everything to a large mixing bowl and add the Parmesan cheese, coating well
6. Then, add the mozzarella and basil and toss once more

Roast Cauliflower & Broccoli

Servings: 6
Cooking Time:xx

Ingredients:

- 300g broccoli
- 300g cauliflower
- 2 tbsp oil
- ½ tsp garlic powder
- ¼ tsp salt
- ¼ tsp paprika
- ⅛ tsp pepper

Directions:

1. Preheat air fryer to 200°C
2. Place broccoli and cauliflower in a bowl and microwave for 3 minutes
3. Add remaining ingredients and mix well
4. Add to the air fryer and cook for about 12 mins

Sweet Potato Taquitos

Servings: 10
Cooking Time:xx

Ingredients:

- 1 sweet potato cut into ½ inch pieces
- 1 ½ tsp oil
- 1 chopped onion
- 1 tsp minced garlic
- 400g black beans
- 3 tbsp water
- 10 corn tortillas
- 1 chipotle pepper, chopped
- ½ tsp cumin
- ½ tsp paprika
- ½ chilli powder
- ⅛ tsp salt
- ½ tsp maple syrup

Directions:

1. Place the sweet potato in the air fryer spray with oil and cook for 12 minutes at 200°C
2. Heat oil in a pan, add the onion and garlic and cook for a few minutes until soft
3. Add remaining ingredients to the pan, add 2 tbsp of water and combine
4. Add the sweet potato and 1 tbsp of water and mix
5. Warm the tortilla in the microwave for about 1 minute
6. Place a row of filling across the centre of each tortilla. Fold up the bottom of the tortilla, tuck under the filling, fold in the edges then continue to roll the tortilla
7. Place in the air fryer and cook for about 12 minutes

Whole Wheat Pizza

Servings: 2
Cooking Time:xx

Ingredients:

- 100g marinara sauce
- 2 whole wheat pitta
- 200g baby spinach leaves
- 1 small plum tomato, sliced
- 1 clove garlic, sliced
- 400g grated cheese
- 50g shaved parmesan

Directions:

1. Preheat air fryer to 160°C
2. Spread each of the pitta with marinara sauce
3. Sprinkle with cheese, top with spinach, plum tomato and garlic. Finish with parmesan shavings
4. Place in the air fryer and cook for about 4 mins cheese has melted

Goat's Cheese Tartlets

Servings: 2
Cooking Time:xx

Ingredients:

- 1 readymade sheet of puff pastry, 35 x 23 cm/14 x 9 in. (gluten-free if you wish)
- 4 tablespoons pesto (jarred or see page 80)
- 4 roasted baby (bell) peppers (see page 120)
- 4 tablespoons soft goat's cheese
- 2 teaspoons milk (plant-based if you wish)

Directions:

1. Cut the pastry sheet in half along the long edge, to make two smaller rectangles. Fold in the edges of each pastry rectangle to form a crust. Using a fork, prick a few holes in the base of the pastry. Brush half the pesto onto each rectangle, top with the peppers and goat's cheese. Brush the pastry crust with milk.
2. Preheat the air-fryer to 180°C/350°F.
3. Place one tartlet on an air-fryer liner or a piece of pierced parchment paper in the preheated air-fryer and air-fry for 6 minutes (you'll need to cook them one at a time). Repeat with the second tartlet.

Spring Ratatouille

Servings:2
Cooking Time:15 Minutes

Ingredients:

- 1 tbsp olive oil
- 4 Roma tomatoes, sliced
- 2 cloves garlic, minced
- 1 courgette, cut into chunks
- 1 red pepper and 1 yellow pepper, cut into chunks
- 2 tbsp mixed herbs
- 1 tbsp vinegar

Directions:

1. Preheat the air fryer to 190 °C / 370 °F and line the air fryer with parchment paper or grease it with olive oil.
2. Place all of the ingredients into a large mixing bowl and mix until fully combined.
3. Transfer the vegetables into the lined air fryer basket, close the lid, and cook for 15 minutes until the vegetables have softened.

Roasted Cauliflower

Servings: 2
Cooking Time:xx

Ingredients:

- 3 cloves garlic
- 1 tbsp peanut oil
- ½ tsp salt
- ½ tsp paprika
- 400g cauliflower florets

Directions:

1. Preheat air fryer to 200°C
2. Crush the garlic, place all ingredients in a bowl and mix well
3. Place in the air fryer and cook for about 15 minutes, shaking every 5 minutes

Lentil Burgers

Servings: 4
Cooking Time:xx

Ingredients:

- 100g black buluga lentils
- 1 carrot, grated
- 1 diced onion
- 100g white cabbage
- 300g oats
- 1 tbsp garlic puree
- 1 tsp cumin
- Salt and pepper

Directions:

1. Blend the oats until they resemble flour
2. Put the lentils in a pan with water and cook for 45 minutes
3. Steam your vegetables for 5 minutes
4. Add all the ingredients into a bowl and mix well to combine
5. Form into burgers place in the air fryer and cook at 180°C for 30 minutes

Baked Potato

Servings: 1
Cooking Time:xx

Ingredients:

- 1 large potato
- 1 tsp oil
- ¼ tsp onion powder
- ⅛ tsp coarse salt
- 1 tbsp of butter
- 1 tbsp of cream cheese
- 1 strip of bacon, diced
- 1 tbsp olives
- 1 tbsp chives

Directions:

1. Pierce the potato in several places with a fork, rub with oil, salt and onion powder
2. Place in the air fryer and cook at 200°C for 35-40 minutes
3. Remove from the air fryer, cut and top with the toppings

Aubergine Dip

Servings: 4
Cooking Time:xx

Ingredients:

- 1 aubergine
- 2 tsp oil
- 3 tbsp tahini
- 1 tbsp lemon juice
- 1 clove garlic minced
- ⅛ tsp cumin
- ¼ tsp smoked salt
- ⅛ tsp salt
- Drizzle olive oil

Directions:

1. Cut the aubergine in half length wise and coat in oil, Place in the air fryer and cook at 200°C for 20 minutes
2. Remove from the air fryer and allow to cool
3. Scoop out the aubergine from the peel and put in a food processor
4. Add all the remaining ingredients, blend to combine but not to a puree
5. Serve with a drizzle of olive oil

Sticky Tofu With Cauliflower Rice

Servings:4
Cooking Time:20 Minutes

Ingredients:

- For the tofu:
- 1 x 180 g / 6 oz block firm tofu
- 2 tbsp soy sauce
- 1 onion, sliced
- 1 large carrot, peeled and thinly sliced
- For the cauliflower:
- 200 g / 7 oz cauliflower florets
- 2 tbsp soy sauce
- 1 tbsp sesame oil
- 2 cloves garlic, minced
- 100 g / 3.5 oz broccoli, chopped into small florets

Directions:

1. Preheat the air fryer to 190 °C / 370 °F and line the air fryer with parchment paper or grease it with olive oil.
2. Crumble the tofu into a bowl and mix in the soy sauce, and the sliced onion and carrot.
3. Cook the tofu and vegetables in the air fryer for 10 minutes.
4. Meanwhile, place the cauliflower florets into a blender and pulse until it forms a rice-like consistency.
5. Place the cauliflower rice in a bowl and mix in the soy sauce, sesame oil, minced garlic cloves, and broccoli florets until well combined. Transfer to the air fryer and cook for 10 minutes until hot and crispy.

Spanakopita Bites

Servings: 4
Cooking Time:xx
Ingredients:

- 300g baby spinach
- 2 tbsp water
- 100g cottage cheese
- 50g feta cheese
- 2 tbsp grated parmesan
- 1 tbsp olive oil
- 4 sheets of filo pastry
- 1 large egg white
- 1 tsp lemon zest
- 1 tsp oregano
- ¼ tsp salt
- ¼ tsp pepper
- ⅛ tsp cayenne

Directions:

1. Place spinach in water and cook for about 5 minutes, drain
2. Mix all ingredients together
3. Place a sheet of pastry down and brush with oil, place another on the top and do the same, continue until all four on top of each other
4. Ut the pastry into 8 strips then cut each strip in half across the middle
5. Add 1 tbsp of mix to each piece of pastry
6. Fold one corner over the mix to create a triangle, fold over the other corner to seal
7. Place in the air fryer and cook at 190°C for about 12 minutes until golden brown

Falafel Burgers

Servings: 2
Cooking Time:xx
Ingredients:

- 1 large can of chickpeas
- 1 onion
- 1 lemon
- 140g oats
- 28g grated cheese
- 28g feta cheese
- Salt and pepper to taste
- 3 tbsp Greek yogurt
- 4 tbsp soft cheese
- 1 tbsp garlic puree
- 1 tbsp coriander
- 1 tbsp oregano
- 1 tbsp parsley

Directions:

1. Place the chickpeas, onion, lemon rind, garlic and seasonings and blend until coarse
2. Add the mix to a bowl and stir in half the soft cheese, cheese and feta
3. Form in to burger shape and coat in the oats
4. Place in the air fryer and cook at 180°C for 8 minutes
5. To make the sauce mix the remaining soft cheese, greek yogurt and lemon juice in a bowl

Crispy Potato Peels

Servings: 1
Cooking Time:xx
Ingredients:

- Peels from 4 potatoes
- Cooking spray
- Salt to season

Directions:

1. Heat the air fryer to 200°C
2. Place the peels in the air fryer spray with oil and sprinkle with salt
3. Cook for about 6-8 minutes until crispy

Broccoli Cheese

Servings: 2
Cooking Time:xx
Ingredients:

- 250g broccoli
- Cooking spray
- 10 tbsp evaporated milk
- 300g Mexican cheese
- 4 tsp Amarillo paste
- 6 saltine crackers

Directions:

1. Heat the air fryer to 190°C
2. Place the broccoli in the air fryer spray with cooking oil and cook for about 6 minutes
3. Place the remaining ingredients in a blender and process until smooth
4. Place in a bowl and microwave for 30 seconds
5. Pour over the broccoli and serve

Arancini

Servings: 12
Cooking Time:xx
Ingredients:

- 1 batch of risotto
- 100g panko breadcrumbs
- 1 tsp onion powder
- Salt and pepper
- 300ml warm marinara sauce

Directions:

1. Take ¼ cup risotto and form a rice ball
2. Mix the panko crumbs, onion powder, salt and pepper
3. Coat the risotto ball in the crumb mix
4. Place in the air fryer, spray with oil and cook at 200°C for 10 minutes
5. Serve with marinara sauce

Orange Zingy Cauliflower

Servings: 2
Cooking Time:xx

Ingredients:

- 200ml water
- 200g flour
- Half the head of a cauliflower, cut into 1.5" florets
- 2 tsp olive oil
- 2 minced garlic cloves
- 1 tsp minced ginger
- 150ml orange juice
- 3 tbsp white vinegar
- 1/2 tsp red pepper flakes
- 1 tsp sesame oil 100g brown sugar
- 3 tbsp soy sauce
- 1 tbsp cornstarch
- 2 tbsp water
- 1 tsp salt

Directions:

1. Take a medium mixing bowl and add the water, salt and flour together
2. Dip each floret of cauliflower into the mixture and place in the air fryer basket
3. Cook at 220°C for 15 minutes
4. Meanwhile make the orange sauce by combining all ingredients in a saucepan and allowing to simmer for 3 minutes, until the sauce has thickened
5. Drizzle the sauce over the cauliflower to serve

Miso Mushrooms On Sourdough Toast

Servings: 1
Cooking Time:xx

Ingredients:

- 1 teaspoon miso paste
- 1 teaspoon oil, such as avocado or coconut (melted)
- 1 teaspoon soy sauce
- 80 g/3 oz. chestnut mushrooms, sliced 5 mm/½ in. thick
- 1 large slice sourdough bread
- 2 teaspoons butter or plant-based spread
- a little freshly chopped flat-leaf parsley, to serve

Directions:

1. Preheat the air-fryer to 200°C/400°F.
2. In a small bowl or ramekin mix together the miso paste, oil and soy sauce.
3. Place the mushrooms in a small shallow gratin dish that fits inside your air-fryer. Add the sauce to the mushrooms and mix together. Place the gratin dish in the preheated air-fryer and air-fry for 6–7 minutes, stirring once during cooking.
4. With 4 minutes left to cook, add the bread to the air-fryer and turn over at 2 minutes whilst giving the mushrooms a final stir.
5. Once cooked, butter the toast and serve the mushrooms on top, scattered with chopped parsley.

Saganaki

Servings: 2

Cooking Time:xx

Ingredients:

- 200 g/7 oz. kefalotyri or manouri cheese, sliced into wedges 1 cm/½ in. thick
- 2 tablespoons plain/all-purpose flour
- olive oil, for drizzling

Directions:

1. Preheat the air-fryer to 200°C/400°F.
2. Dip each wedge of cheese in the flour, then tap off any excess. Drizzle olive oil onto both sides of the cheese slices
3. Add the cheese to the preheated air-fryer and air-fry for 3 minutes. Remove from the air-fryer and serve.

Veggie Bakes

Servings: 2

Cooking Time:xx

Ingredients:

- Any type of leftover vegetable bake you have
- 30g flour

Directions:

1. Preheat the air fryer to 180°C
2. Mix the flour with the leftover vegetable bake
3. Shape into balls and place in the air fryer
4. Cook for 10 minutes

Artichoke Pasta

Servings: 2

Cooking Time:xx

Ingredients:

- 100g pasta
- 50g basil leaves
- 6 artichoke hearts
- 2 tbsp pumpkin seeds
- 2 tbsp lemon juice
- 1 clove garlic
- ½ tsp white miso paste
- 1 can chickpeas
- 1 tsp olive oil

Directions:

1. Place the chickpeas in the air fryer and cook at 200°C for 12 minutes
2. Cook the pasta according to packet instructions
3. Add the remaining ingredients to a food processor and blend
4. Add the pasta to a bowl and spoon over the pesto mix
5. Serve and top with roasted chickpeas

Spinach And Egg Air Fryer Breakfast Muffins

Servings:4
Cooking Time:10 Minutes

Ingredients:

- 8 eggs
- 100 g / 3.5 oz fresh spinach
- 50 g / 1.8 oz cheddar cheese, grated
- ½ onion, finely sliced
- 1 tsp black pepper

Directions:

1. Preheat your air fryer to 200 °C / 400 °F and line an 8-pan muffin tray with parchment paper or grease with olive oil.
2. Gently press the spinach leaves into the bottom of each prepared muffin cup.
3. Sprinkle the finely sliced onion on top of the spinach.
4. Crack 2 eggs into each cup on top of the spinach and add some of the grated cheddar cheese on top of the eggs. Top with a light sprinkle of black pepper.
5. Carefully place the muffins into the air fryer basket and shut the lid. Bake for 10 minutes until the eggs are set and the muffins are hot throughout.
6. Serve the muffins while still hot for breakfast.

Tomato And Herb Tofu

Servings:4
Cooking Time:10 Minutes

Ingredients:

- 1 x 400 g / 14 oz block firm tofu
- 1 tbsp soy sauce
- 2 tbsp tomato paste
- 1 tsp dried oregano
- 1 tsp dried basil
- 1 tsp garlic powder

Directions:

1. Remove the tofu from the packaging and place on a sheet of kitchen roll. Place another sheet of kitchen roll on top of the tofu and place a plate on top of it.
2. Use something heavy to press the plate down on top of the tofu. Leave for 10 minutes to press the water out of the tofu.
3. Remove the paper towels from the tofu and chop them into even slices that are around ½ cm thick.
4. Preheat the air fryer to 180 °C / 350 °F. Remove the mesh basket from the air fryer machine and line with parchment paper.
5. Place the tofu slices on a lined baking sheet.
6. In a bowl, mix the soy sauce, tomato paste, dried oregano, dried basil, and garlic powder until fully combined.
7. Spread the mixture evenly over the tofu slices. Place the tofu slices on the baking sheet in the lined air fryer basket and cook for 10 minutes until the tofu is firm and crispy.
8. Serve the tofu slices with a side of rice or noodles and some hot vegetables.

Rainbow Vegetables

Servings: 4
Cooking Time:xx
Ingredients:

- 1 red pepper, cut into slices
- 1 squash sliced
- 1 courgette sliced
- 1 tbsp olive oil
- 150g sliced mushrooms
- 1 onion sliced
- Salt and pepper to taste

Directions:

1. Preheat air fryer to 180°C
2. Place all ingredients in a bowl and mix well
3. Place in the air fryer and cook for about 20 minutes turning halfway

Butternut Squash Falafel

Servings: 2
Cooking Time:xx
Ingredients:

- 500 g/1 lb. 2 oz. frozen butternut squash cubes
- 1 tablespoon olive oil, plus extra for cooking
- 100 g/¾ cup canned or cooked chickpeas (drained weight)
- 20 g/¼ cup gram/chickpea flour
- 1 teaspoon ground cumin
- ½ teaspoon ground coriander
- ½ teaspoon salt

Directions:

1. Preheat the air-fryer to 180°C/350°F.
2. Toss the frozen butternut squash in the olive oil. Add to the preheated air-fryer and air-fry for 12–14 minutes, until soft but not caramelized. Remove from the air-fryer and mash the squash by hand or using a food processor, then combine with the chickpeas, flour, spices and salt. Leave the mixture to cool, then divide into 6 equal portions and mould into patties.
3. Preheat the air-fryer to 180°C/350°F.
4. Spray the patties with a little olive oil, then add to the preheated air-fryer and air-fry for 10 minutes, turning once (carefully) during cooking. Enjoy hot or cold.

Air Fryer Cheese Sandwich

Servings:2
Cooking Time:10 Minutes
Ingredients:

- 4 slices white or wholemeal bread
- 2 tbsp butter
- 50 g / 3.5 oz cheddar cheese, grated

Directions:

1. Preheat the air fryer to 180 °C / 350 °F and line the bottom of the basket with parchment paper.
2. Lay the slices of bread out on a clean surface and butter one side of each. Evenly sprinkle the cheese on two of the slices and cover with the final two slices.
3. Transfer the sandwiches to the air fryer, close the lid, and cook for 5 minutes until the bread is crispy and golden, and the cheese is melted.

Radish Hash Browns

Servings: 4
Cooking Time:xx

Ingredients:

- 300g radish
- 1 onion
- 1 tsp onion powder
- ¾ tsp sea salt
- ½ tsp paprika
- ¼ tsp ground black pepper
- 1 tsp coconut oil

Directions:

1. Wash the radish, trim off the roots and slice in a processor along with the onions
2. Add the coconut oil and mix well
3. Put the onions and radish into the air fryer and cook at 180°C for 8 minutes shaking a few times
4. Put the onion and radish in a bowl add seasoning and mix well
5. Put back in the air fryer and cook at 200°C for 5 minutes

Tempura Veggies

Servings: 4
Cooking Time:xx

Ingredients:

- 150g flour
- ½ tsp salt
- ½ tsp pepper
- 2 eggs
- 2 tbsp cup water
- 100g avocado wedges
- 100g courgette slices
- 100g panko breadcrumbs
- 2 tsp oil
- 100g green beans
- 100g asparagus spears
- 100g red onion rings
- 100g pepper rings

Directions:

1. Mix together flour, salt and pepper. In another bowl mix eggs and water
2. Stir together panko crumbs and oil in a separate bowl
3. Dip vegetables in the flour mix, then egg and then the bread crumbs
4. Preheat the air fryer to 200°C
5. Place in the air fryer and cook for about 10 minutes until golden brown

Beef & Lamb And Pork Recipes

Japanese Pork Chops

Servings: 4
Cooking Time:xx
Ingredients:

- 6 boneless pork chops
- 30g flour
- 2 beaten eggs
- 2 tbsp sweet chilli sauce
- 500g cup seasoned breadcrumbs
- ⅛ tsp salt
- ⅛ tsp pepper
- Tonkatsu sauce to taste

Directions:

1. Place the flour, breadcrumbs and eggs in 3 separate bowls
2. Sprinkle both sides of the pork with salt and pepper
3. Coat the pork in flour, egg and then breadcrumbs
4. Place in the air fryer and cook at 180°C for 8 minutes, turn then cook for a further 5 minutes
5. Serve with sauces on the side

Steak Dinner

Servings: 5
Cooking Time:xx
Ingredients:

- 400g sirloin steak, cut into cubes
- 300g red potatoes, cubed
- 1 pepper
- 1 tsp dried parsley
- ½ tsp pepper
- 2 tsp olive oil
- 1 sliced onion
- 300g chopped mushrooms
- 2 tsp garlic salt
- 2 tsp salt
- 5 tsp butter

Directions:

1. Preheat the air fryer to 200°C
2. Take 5 pieces of foil, layer meat onion, potatoes, mushrooms and pepper in each one
3. Add 1 tsp of butter to each one
4. Mix seasonings and sprinkle over the top
5. Fold the foil and cook for 25-30 minutes

Salt And Pepper Belly Pork

Servings: 4
Cooking Time:xx

Ingredients:

- 500g belly pork
- 1 tsp pepper
- ½ tsp salt

Directions:

1. Cut the pork into bite size pieces and season with salt and pepper
2. Heat the air fryer to 200°C
3. Place in the air fryer and cook for 15 minutes until crisp

Sticky Asian Beef

Servings: 2
Cooking Time:xx

Ingredients:

- 1 tbsp coconut oil
- 2 sliced peppers
- 25g liquid aminos
- 25g cup water
- 100g brown sugar
- ¼ tsp pepper
- ½ tsp ground ginger
- ½ tbsp minced garlic
- 1 tsp red pepper flakes
- 600g steak thinly sliced
- ¼ tsp salt

Directions:

1. Melt the coconut oil in a pan, add the peppers and cook until softened
2. In another pan add the aminos, brown sugar, ginger, garlic and pepper flakes. Mix and bring to the boil, simmer for 10 mins
3. Season the steak with salt and pepper
4. Put the steak in the air fryer and cook at 200°C for 10 minutes. Turn the steak and cook for a further 5 minutes until crispy
5. Add the steak to the peppers then mix with the sauce
6. Serve with rice

Jamaican Jerk Pork

Servings: 4
Cooking Time:xx

Ingredients:

- 400g pork butt cut into 3 pieces
- 100g jerk paste

Directions:

1. Rub the pork with jerk paste and marinate for 4 hours
2. Preheat air fryer to 190°C
3. Place pork in the air fryer and cook for about 20 minutes turning halfway

Old Fashioned Steak

Servings: 4
Cooking Time:xx

Ingredients:

- 4 medium steaks
- 100g flour
- ½ tsp garlic powder
- Salt and pepper
- 1 egg
- 4 slices bacon
- 350ml milk

Directions:

1. Beat the egg
2. Mix the flour with garlic powder, salt and pepper
3. Dip the steak into the egg then cover in the flour mix
4. Place in the air fryer and cook at 170°C for 7 minutes, turnover and cook for another 10 minutes until golden brown
5. Whilst the steak is cooking, place the bacon in a frying pan, stir in the flour. Add milk to the bacon and stir until there are no lumps in the flour
6. Season with salt and pepper Cook for 2 minutes until thickened season with salt and pepper

Beef Satay

Servings: 2
Cooking Time:xx

Ingredients:

- 400g steak strips
- 2 tbsp oil
- 1 tbsp fish sauce
- 1 tsp sriracha sauce
- 200g sliced coriander (fresh)
- 1 tsp ground coriander
- 1 tbsp soy
- 1 tbsp minced ginger
- 1 tbsp minced garlic
- 1 tbsp sugar
- 25g roasted peanuts

Directions:

1. Add oil, dish sauce, soy, ginger, garlic, sugar sriracha, coriander and ¼ cup coriander to a bowl and mix. Add the steak and marinate for 30 minutes
2. Add the steak to the air fryer and cook at 200°C for about 8 minutes
3. Place the steak on a plate and top with remaining coriander and chopped peanuts
4. Serve with peanut sauce

Beef Bulgogi Burgers

Servings: 4
Cooking Time:xx
Ingredients:

- 500g minced beef
- 2 tbsp gochujang
- 1 tbsp soy
- 2 tsp minced garlic
- 2 tsp minced ginger
- 2 tsp sugar
- 1 tbsp olive oil
- 1 chopped onion

Directions:

1. Mix all the ingredients in a large bowl, allow to rest for at least 30 minutes in the fridge
2. Divide the meat into four and form into patties
3. Place in the air fryer and cook at 180°C for about 10 minutes
4. Serve in burger buns, if desired

Traditional Empanadas

Servings: 2
Cooking Time:xx
Ingredients:

- 300g minced beef
- 1 tbsp olive oil
- ¼ cup finely chopped onion
- 150g chopped mushrooms
- ⅛ tsp cinnamon
- 4 chopped tomatoes
- 2 tsp chopped garlic
- 6 green olives
- ¼ tsp paprika
- ¼ tsp cumin
- 8 goyoza wrappers
- 1 beaten egg

Directions:

1. Heat oil in a pan add onion and minced beef and cook until browned
2. Add mushrooms and cook for 6 minutes
3. Add garlic, olives, paprika, cumin and cinnamon, and cook for about 3 minutes
4. Stir in tomatoes and cook for 1 minute, set aside allow to cool
5. Place 1 ½ tbsp of filling in each goyoza wrapper
6. Brush edges with egg fold over and seal pinching edges
7. Place in the air fryer and cook at 200 for about 7 minutes

Steak And Mushrooms

Servings: 4
Cooking Time:xx

Ingredients:

- 500g cubed sirloin steak
- 300g button mushrooms
- 3 tbsp Worcestershire sauce
- 1 tbsp olive oil
- 1 tsp parsley flakes
- 1 tsp paprika
- 1 tsp crushed chilli flakes

Directions:

1. Combine all ingredients in a bowl, cover and chill for at least 4 hours
2. Preheat air fryer to 200°C
3. Drain and discard the marinade from the steak
4. Place the steak and mushrooms in the air fryer and cook for 5 minutes
5. Toss and cook for a further 5 minutes

Pulled Pork, Bacon, And Cheese Sliders

Servings:2
Cooking Time:30 Minutes

Ingredients:

- 2 x 50 g / 3.5 oz pork steaks
- 1 tsp salt
- 1 tsp black pepper
- 4 slices bacon strips, chopped into small pieces
- 1 tbsp soy sauce
- 1 tbsp BBQ sauce
- 100 g / 7 oz cheddar cheese, grated
- 2 bread buns

Directions:

1. Preheat the air fryer to 200 °C / 400 °F and line the bottom of the basket with parchment paper.
2. Place the pork steaks on a clean surface and season with salt and black pepper. Move the pork steak in the prepared air fryer basket and cook for 15 minutes.
3. Remove the steak from the air fryer and shred using two forks. Mix with the chopped bacon in a heatproof bowl and place the bowl in the air fryer. Cook for 10 minutes.
4. Remove the bowl from the air fryer and stir in the soy sauce and BBQ sauce. Return the bowl to the air fryer basket and continue cooking for a further 5 minutes.
5. Meanwhile, spread the cheese across one half of the bread buns. Top with the cooked pulled pork and an extra squirt of BBQ sauce.

Beef Stirfry

Servings: 2
Cooking Time:xx
Ingredients:

- 500g steak
- 400g broccoli
- 3 peppers, cut into strips
- 1 tbsp ground ginger
- 25ml water
- 1 sliced onion
- 25g hoisin sauce
- 2 tsp minced garlic
- 1 tsp sesame oil
- 1 tbsp soy

Directions:

1. Add sesame oil, hoisin sauce, garlic, soy and water to a bowl and then add the steak, allow to marinate for 20 minutes
2. Mix 1 tbsp of oil with the vegetables and place in the air fryer, cook at 200°C for about 5 minutes
3. Place the vegetables in a bowl and put aside
4. Add meat to air fryer and cook for 4 minutes, turn and cook for a further 2 minutes
5. Mix the steak with the vegetables and serve with rice

Pork Chops With Raspberry And Balsamic

Servings: 4
Cooking Time:xx
Ingredients:

- 2 large eggs
- 30ml milk
- 250g panko bread crumbs
- 250g finely chopped pecans
- 1 tbsp orange juice
- 4 pork chops
- 30ml balsamic vinegar
- 2 tbsp brown sugar
- 2 tbsp raspberry jam

Directions:

1. Preheat air fryer to 200°C
2. Mix the eggs and milk together in a bowl
3. In another bowl mix the breadcrumbs and pecans
4. Coat the pork chops in flour, egg and then coat in the breadcrumbs
5. Place in the air fryer and cook for 12 minutes until golden turning halfway
6. Put the remaining ingredients in a pan simmer for about 6 minutes, serve with the pork chops

Pork With Chinese 5 Spice

Servings: 4
Cooking Time:xx

Ingredients:

- 2 pork rounds cut into chunks
- 2 large eggs
- 1 tsp sesame oil
- 200g cornstarch
- 1/4 tsp salt
- ½ tsp pepper
- 3 tbsp canola oil
- 1 tsp Chinese 5 spice

Directions:

1. In a bowl mix the corn starch, salt, pepper and 5 spice
2. Mix the eggs and sesame oil in another bowl
3. Dip the pork into the egg and then cover in the corn starch mix
4. Place in the air fryer and cook at 170°C for 11-12 minutes, shaking halfway through
5. Serve with sweet and sour sauce

Hamburgers With Feta

Servings: 4
Cooking Time:xx

Ingredients:

- 400g minced beef
- 250g crumbled feta
- 25g chopped green olives
- ½ tsp garlic powder
- ½ cup chopped onion
- 2 tbsp Worcestershire sauce
- ½ tsp steak seasoning
- Salt to taste

Directions:

1. Mix all the ingredients in a bowl
2. Divide the mix into four and shape into patties
3. Place in the air fryer and cook at 200°C for about 15 minutes

Hamburgers

Servings: 4
Cooking Time:xx

Ingredients:

- 500g minced beef
- 1 grated onion
- Salt and pepper to taste

Directions:

1. Preheat air fryer to 200°C
2. Place the grated onion and the beef into a bowl and combine together well
3. Divide minced beef into 4 equal portions, form into patties
4. Season with salt and pepper
5. Place in the air fryer and cook for 10 minutes, turnover and cook for a further 3 minutes

Beef And Cheese Empanadas

Servings: 12
Cooking Time:xx
Ingredients:

- 2 tsp oil
- 1 chopped onion
- 1 clove chopped garlic
- 500g minced beef
- Salt and pepper
- 2 tbsp chopped jalapeño
- 2 packs ready made pastry
- 50g grated cheddar cheese
- 50g pepper jack cheese
- 1 egg

Directions:

1. Heat the oil in a pan and fry the onion and garlic until soft
2. Add the meat and jalapeño, season with salt and pepper, and cook until browned
3. Allow the meat to cool
4. Roll out dough as thin as possible and cut into circles, fill with 1 tablespoon of mix, sprinkle with cheese, fold over and seal with the egg
5. Set your fryer to 170°C and cook for about 12 minutes until golden brown

Beef Stuffed Peppers

Servings: 4
Cooking Time:xx
Ingredients:

- 4 bell peppers
- ½ chopped onion
- 1 minced garlic clove
- 500g minced beef
- 5 tbsp tomato sauce
- 100g grated cheese
- 2 tsp Worcestershire sauce
- 1 tsp garlic powder
- A pinch of black pepper
- ½ tsp chilli powder
- 1 tsp dried basil
- 75g cooked rice

Directions:

1. Cook the onions, minced beef, garlic and all the seasonings until the meat is browned
2. Remove from the heat and add Worcestershire sauce, rice, ½ the cheese and ⅔ of the tomato sauce mix well
3. Cut the tops off the peppers and remove the seeds
4. Stuff the peppers with the mixture and place in the air fryer
5. Cook at 200°C for about 11 minutes
6. When there are 3 minutes remaining top the peppers with the rest of the tomato sauce and cheese

Tahini Beef Bites

Servings: 2
Cooking Time:xx

Ingredients:

- 500g sirloin steak, cut into cubes
- 2 tbsp Za'atar seasoning
- 1 tsp olive oil
- 25g Tahini
- 25g warm water
- 1 tbsp lemon juice
- 1 clove of garlic
- Salt to taste

Directions:

1. Preheat the air fryer to 250°C
2. Take a bowl and combine the oil with the steak, salt, and Za'atar seasoning
3. Place in the air fryer and cook for 10 minutes, turning halfway through
4. Take a bowl and combine the water, garlic, lemon juice, salt, and tahini, or use a food processor if you have one
5. Pour the sauce over the bites and serve

Butter Steak & Asparagus

Servings: 6
Cooking Time:xx

Ingredients:

- 500g steak, cut into 6 pieces
- Salt and pepper
- 75g tamari sauce
- 2 cloves crushed garlic
- 400g asparagus
- 3 sliced peppers
- 25g balsamic vinegar
- 50g beef broth
- 2 tbsp butter

Directions:

1. Season steaks with salt and pepper
2. Place steaks in a bowl, add tamari sauce and garlic make sure steaks are covered, leave to marinate for at least 1hr
3. Place steaks on a board, fill with peppers and asparagus, roll the steak around and secure with tooth picks
4. Set your fryer to 200°C and cook for 5 minutes.
5. Whilst cooking heat the broth, butter and balsamic vinegar in a saucepan until thickened
6. Pour over the steaks and serve

Sausage Gnocchi One Pot

Servings: 2
Cooking Time:xx

Ingredients:

- 4 links of sausage
- 250g green beans, washed and cut into halves
- 1 tsp Italian seasoning
- 1 tbsp olive oil
- 300g gnocchi
- Salt and pepper for seasoning

Directions:

1. Preheat the air fryer to 220°C
2. Cut the sausage up into pieces
3. Take a bowl and add the gnocchi and green beans, along with the oil and season
4. Place the sausage into the fryer first and then the rest of the ingredients
5. Cook for 12 minutes, giving everything a stir halfway through

Homemade Crispy Pepperoni Pizza

Servings:4
Cooking Time:10 Minutes

Ingredients:

- For the pizza dough:
- 500 g / 17.6 oz plain flour
- 1 tsp salt
- 1 tsp dry non-fast-acting yeast
- 400 ml warm water
- For the toppings:
- 100 g / 3.5 oz tomato sauce
- 100 g / 3.5 oz mozzarella cheese, grated
- 8 slices pepperoni

Directions:

1. To make the pizza dough, place the plain flour, salt, and dry yeast in a large mixing bowl. Pour in the warm water bit by bit until it forms a tacky dough.
2. Lightly dust a clean kitchen top surface with plain flour and roll the dough out until it is around ½ an inch thick.
3. Preheat your air fryer to 150 °C / 300 °F and line the bottom of the basket with parchment paper.
4. Spread the tomato sauce evenly across the dough and top with grated mozzarella cheese. Top with the pepperoni slices and carefully transfer the pizza into the lined air fryer basket.
5. Cook the pizza until the crust is golden and crispy, and the mozzarella cheese has melted.
6. Enjoy the pizza while still hot with a side salad and some potato wedges.

Mustard Pork Tenderloin

Servings: 2
Cooking Time:xx
Ingredients:

- 1 pork tenderloin
- 3 tbsp soy sauce
- 2 minced garlic cloves
- 3 tbsp olive oil
- 2 tbsp brown sugar
- 1 tbsp dijon mustard
- Salt and pepper for seasoning

Directions:

1. Take a bowl and combine the ingredients, except for the pork
2. Pour the mixture into a ziplock bag and then add the pork
3. Close the top and make sure the pork is well covered
4. Place in the refrigerator for 30minutes
5. Preheat your air fryer to 260°C
6. Remove the pork from the bag and place in the fryer
7. Cook for 25 minutes, turning halfway
8. Remove and rest for 5 minutes before slicing into pieces

Cheesy Beef Enchiladas

Servings: 4
Cooking Time:xx
Ingredients:

- 500g minced beef
- 1 packet taco seasoning
- 8 tortillas
- 300g grated cheese
- 150g soured cream
- 1 can black beans
- 1 can chopped tomatoes
- 1 can mild chopped chillies
- 1 can red enchilada sauce
- 300g chopped coriander

Directions:

1. Brown the beef and add the taco seasoning
2. Add the beef, beans, tomatoes and chillies to the tortillas
3. Line the air fryer with foil and put the tortillas in
4. Pour the enchilada sauce over the top and sprinkle with cheese
5. Cook at 200°C for five minutes, remove from air fryer add toppings and serve

Steak Popcorn Bites

Servings: 4
Cooking Time:xx

Ingredients:

- 500g steak, cut into 1" sized cubes
- 500g potato chips, ridged ones work best
- 100g flour
- 2 beaten eggs
- Salt and pepper to taste

Directions:

1. Place the chips into the food processor and pulse unit you get fine chip crumbs
2. Take a bowl and combine the flour with salt and pepper
3. Add the chips to another bowl and the beaten egg to another bowl
4. Take the steak cubes and dip first in the flour, then the egg and then the chip crumbs
5. Preheat your air fryer to 260°C
6. Place the steak pieces into the fryer and cook for 9 minutes

Crispy Chili Sausages

Servings:4
Cooking Time:20 Minutes

Ingredients:

- 8 sausages, uncooked
- 2 eggs
- ½ tsp salt
- ½ black pepper
- ½ tsp chili flakes
- ½ tsp paprika

Directions:

1. Preheat the air fryer to 180 °C / 350 °F and line the bottom of the basket with parchment paper.
2. Place the sausages in the air fryer and cook for 5 minutes until slightly browned, but not fully cooked. Remove from the air fryer and set aside.
3. While the sausages are cooking, whisk together the eggs, salt, black pepper, chili flakes, and paprika. Coat the sausages evenly in the egg and spice mixture.
4. Return the sausages to the air fryer and cook for a further 5 minutes until brown and crispy.
5. Eat the sausages while hot with a side of steamed vegetables or place them in a sandwich for lunch.

Pork Taquitos

Servings: 5
Cooking Time:xx

Ingredients:

- 400g shredded pork
- 500g grated mozzarella
- 10 flour tortillas
- The juice of 1 lime
- Cooking spray

Directions:

1. Preheat air fryer to 190°C
2. Sprinkle lime juice on the pork and mix
3. Microwave tortilla for about 10 seconds to soften
4. Add a little pork and cheese to a tortilla
5. Roll then tortilla up, and place in the air fryer
6. Cook for about 7 minutes until golden, turn halfway through cooking

Char Siu Buffalo

Servings: 2
Cooking Time:xx

Ingredients:

- 1 kg beef, cut into strips
- 4 tbsp honey
- 2 tbsp sugar
- 2 tbsp char siu sauce
- 2 tbsp oyster sauce
- 2 tbsp soy sauce
- 2 tbsp olive oil
- 2 tsp minced garlic
- ¼ tsp bi carbonate of soda

Directions:

1. Place all the ingredients in a bowl, mix well and marinate over night
2. Line the air fryer with foil, add the beef, keep the marinade to one side
3. Cook at 200°C for 10 minutes
4. Brush the pork with the sauce and cook for another 20 minutes at 160°C
5. Remove the meat and set aside
6. Strain the marinade into a saucepan, heat until it thickens
7. Drizzle over the pork and serve with rice

Copycat Burger

Servings: 4
Cooking Time:xx

Ingredients:

- 400g minced pork
- 4 wholemeal burger buns
- Avocado sauce to taste
- 1 avocado
- 1 small onion, chopped
- 2 chopped spring onions
- Salad garnish
- 1 tbsp Worcester sauce
- 1 tbsp tomato ketchup
- 1 tsp garlic puree
- 1 tsp mixed herbs

Directions:

1. In a bowl mix together the mince, onion, half the avocado and all of the seasoning
2. Form into burgers
3. Place in the air fryer and cook at 180°C for 8 minutes
4. When cooked place in the bun, layer with sauce and salad garnish

Chinese Chilli Beef

Servings: 2
Cooking Time:xx

Ingredients:

- 4 tbsp light soy sauce
- 1 tsp honey
- 3 tbsp tomato ketchup
- 1 tsp Chinese 5 spice
- 1 tbsp oil
- 6 tbsp sweet chilli sauce
- 1 tbsp lemon juice
- 400g frying steak
- 2 tbsp cornflour

Directions:

1. Slice the steak into strips, put into a bowl and cover with cornflour and 5 spice
2. Add to the air fryer and cook for 6 minutes at 200°C
3. Whilst the beef is cooking mix together the remaining ingredients
4. Add to the air fryer and cook for another 3 minutes

Asian Meatballs

Servings: 2
Cooking Time:xx

Ingredients:

- 500g minced pork
- 2 eggs
- 100g breadcrumbs
- 1 tsp minced garlic
- ⅓ tsp chilli flakes
- 1 tsp minced ginger
- 1 tsp sesame oil
- 1 tsp soy
- 2 diced spring onions
- Salt and pepper to taste

Directions:

1. Mix all ingredients in a bowl until combined
2. Form mix into 1 ½ inch meatballs
3. Place in the air fryer and cook at 200°C for about 10 minutes until cooked

Beef Nacho Pinwheels

Servings: 6
Cooking Time:xx

Ingredients:

- 500g minced beef
- 1 packet of taco seasoning
- 300ml water
- 300ml sour cream
- 6 tostadas
- 6 flour tortillas

- 3 tomatoes
- 250g nacho cheese
- 250g shredded lettuce
- 250g Mexican cheese

Directions:

1. Preheat air fryer to 200°C
2. Brown the mince in a pan and add the taco seasoning
3. Share the remaining ingredients between the tortillas
4. Fold the edges of the tortillas up towards the centre, should look like a pinwheel
5. Lay seam down in the air fryer and cook for 2 minutes
6. Turnover and cook for a further 2 minutes

Cheese & Ham Sliders

Servings: 4
Cooking Time:xx

Ingredients:

- 8 slider bread rolls, cut in half
- 16 slices of sweet ham
- 16 slices of Swiss cheese
- 5 tbsp mayonnaise
- 1/2 tsp paprika
- 1 tsp onion powder
- 1 tsp dill

Directions:

1. Place 2 slices of ham into each bread roll and 2 slices of cheese
2. Take a bowl and combine the mayonnaise with the onion powder, dill and paprika
3. Add half a tablespoon of the sauce on top of each piece of cheese
4. Place the top on the bread slider
5. Cook at 220°C for 5 minutes

Beef Stroganoff

Servings:4
Cooking Time:20 Minutes

Ingredients:

- 4 cubes / 800 ml beef stock cubes
- 4 tbsp olive oil
- 1 onion, chopped
- 200 g / 7 oz sour cream
- 200 g / 7 oz mushroom, finely sliced
- 500 g / 17.6 oz steak, chopped
- 4 x 100 g / 3.5 oz egg noodles, cooked

Directions:

1. Preheat the air fryer to 200 °C / 400 °F and line the bottom of the basket with parchment paper.
2. Boil 800 ml of water and use it to dissolve the 4 beef stock cubes.
3. In a heat-proof bowl, mix the olive oil, onion, sour cream, mushrooms, and beef stock until fully combined.
4. Coat all sides of the steak chunks in the mixture and set aside to marinate for 10 minutes.
5. Transfer the steak to the air fryer, close the lid, and cook for 10 minutes. Serve the steak hot with a serving of egg noodles.

Fish & Seafood Recipes

Thai-style Tuna Fishcakes

Servings: 2
Cooking Time:xx
Ingredients:

- 200 g/7 oz. cooked potato
- 145 g/5 oz. canned tuna, drained
- 60 g/1 cup canned sweetcorn/corn kernels (drained weight)
- ½ teaspoon soy sauce
- ½ teaspoon fish sauce
- ½ teaspoon Thai 7 spice
- freshly squeezed juice of ½ a lime
- 1 teaspoon freshly grated garlic
- 1 teaspoon freshly grated ginger
- avocado or olive oil, for brushing
- LIME-ALMOND SATAY SAUCE
- 20 ml/4 teaspoons fresh lime juice
- 2 heaped tablespoons almond butter
- 1 teaspoon soy sauce
- ½ teaspoon freshly grated ginger
- ½ teaspoon freshly grated garlic
- ½ teaspoon avocado or olive oil
- ½ teaspoon maple syrup

Directions:

1. Combine all the fishcake ingredients in a food processor and blend together. Divide the mixture into 6 equal portions and mould into fishcakes. Brush a little oil over the top surface of the fishcakes.
2. Preheat the air-fryer to 180°C/350°F.
3. Place the fishcakes on an air-fryer liner or a piece of pierced parchment paper and add to the preheated air-fryer. Air-fry for 4 minutes, then turn over and brush the other side of each fishcake with oil and air-fry for a further 4 minutes.
4. To make the satay dipping sauce, mix all ingredients in a bowl with 1 tablespoon warm water. Serve alongside the fishcakes.

Salmon Patties

Servings: 4
Cooking Time:xx
Ingredients:

- 400g salmon
- 1 egg
- 1 diced onion
- 200g breadcrumbs
- 1 tsp dill weed

Directions:

1. Remove all bones and skin from the salmon
2. Mix egg, onion, dill weed and bread crumbs with the salmon
3. Shape mixture into patties and place into the air fryer
4. Set air fryer to 180°C
5. Cook for 5 minutes then turn them over and cook for a further 5 minutes until golden brown

Fish In Foil

Servings: 2
Cooking Time:xx

Ingredients:

- 1 tablespoon avocado oil or olive oil, plus extra for greasing
- 1 tablespoon soy sauce (or tamari)
- 1½ teaspoons freshly grated garlic
- 1½ teaspoons freshly grated ginger
- 1 small red chilli/chile, finely chopped
- 2 skinless, boneless white fish fillets (about 350 g/12 oz. total weight)

Directions:

1. Mix the oil, soy sauce, garlic, ginger and chilli/chile together. Brush a little oil onto two pieces of foil, then lay the fish in the centre of the foil. Spoon the topping mixture over the fish. Wrap the foil around the fish to make a parcel, with a gap above the fish but shallow enough to fit in your air-fryer basket.
2. Preheat the air-fryer to 180°C/350°F.
3. Add the foil parcels to the preheated air-fryer and air-fry for 7–10 minutes, depending on the thickness of your fillets. The fish should just flake when a fork is inserted. Serve immediately.

Thai Salmon Patties

Servings: 7
Cooking Time:xx

Ingredients:

- 1 large can of salmon, drained and bones removed
- 30g panko breadcrumbs
- ¼ tsp salt
- 1 ½ tbsp Thai red curry paste
- 1 ½ tbsp brown sugar
- Zest of 1 lime
- 2 eggs
- Cooking spray

Directions:

1. Take a large bowl and combine all ingredients together until smooth
2. Use your hands to create patties that are around 1 inch in thickness
3. Preheat your air fryer to 180°C
4. Coat the patties with cooking spray
5. Cook for 4 minutes each side

Air Fried Scallops

Servings: 2
Cooking Time:xx

Ingredients:

- 6 scallops
- 1 tbsp olive oil
- Salt and pepper to taste

Directions:

1. Brush the filets with olive oil
2. Sprinkle with salt and pepper
3. Place in the air fryer and cook at 200°C for 2 mins
4. Turn the scallops over and cook for another 2 minutes

Coconut Shrimp

Servings: 4
Cooking Time:xx

Ingredients:

- 250g flour
- 1 ½ tsp black pepper
- 2 eggs
- 150g unsweetened flaked coconut
- 1 Serrano chilli, thinly sliced
- 25g panko bread crumbs
- 300g shrimp raw
- ½ tsp salt
- 4 tbsp honey
- 25ml lime juice

Directions:

1. Mix together flour and pepper, in another bowl beat the eggs and in another bowl mix the panko and coconut
2. Dip each of the shrimp in the flour mix then the egg and then cover in the coconut mix
3. Coat the shrimp in cooking spray
4. Place in the air fryer and cook at 200°C for 6-8 mins turning half way through
5. Mix together the honey, lime juice and chilli and serve with the shrimp

Thai Fish Cakes

Servings: 4
Cooking Time:xx

Ingredients:

- 200g pre-mashed potatoes
- 2 fillets of white fish, flaked and mashed
- 1 onion
- 1 tsp butter
- 1 tsp milk
- 1 lime zest and rind
- 3 tsp chilli
- 1 tsp Worcester sauce
- 1 tsp coriander
- 1 tsp mixed spice
- 1 tsp mixed herbs
- 50g breadcrumbs
- Salt and pepper to taste

Directions:

1. Cover the white fish in milk
2. in a mixing bowl place the fish and add the seasoning and mashed potatoes
3. Add the butter and remaining milk
4. Use your hands to create patties and place in the refrigerator for 3 hours
5. Preheat your air fryer to 200°C
6. Cook for 15 minutes

Air Fryer Tuna

Servings: 2
Cooking Time:xx

Ingredients:

- 2 tuna steaks, boneless and skinless
- 2 tsp honey
- 1 tsp grated ginger
- 4 tbsp soy sauce
- 1 tsp sesame oil
- 1/2 tsp rice vinegar

Directions:

1. Combine the honey, soy sauce, rice vinegar and sesame oil in a bowl until totally mixed together
2. Cover the tuna steaks with the sauce and place in the refrigerator for half an hour to marinade
3. Preheat the air fryer to 270°C
4. Cook the tuna for 4 minutes
5. Allow to rest before slicing

Cajun Prawn Skewers

Servings: 2
Cooking Time:xx

Ingredients:

- 350 g/12 oz. king prawns/jumbo shrimp
- MARINADE
- 1 teaspoon smoked paprika
- 1 teaspoon unrefined sugar
- 1 teaspoon salt
- ½ teaspoon onion powder
- ½ teaspoon mustard powder
- ¼ teaspoon dried oregano
- ¼ teaspoon dried thyme
- 1 teaspoon white wine vinegar
- 2 teaspoons olive oil

Directions:

1. Mix all the marinade ingredients together in a bowl. Mix the prawns/shrimp into the marinade and cover. Place in the fridge to marinate for at least an hour.
2. Preheat the air-fryer to 180°C/350°F.
3. Thread 4–5 prawns/shrimp on to each skewer (you should have enough for 4–5 skewers). Add the skewers to the preheated air-fryer and air fry for 2 minutes, then turn the skewers and cook for a further 2 minutes. Check the internal temperature of the prawns/shrimp has reached at least 50°C/125°F using a meat thermometer – if not, cook for another few minutes. Serve immediately.

Traditional Fish And Chips

Servings: 4
Cooking Time:xx

Ingredients:

- 4 potatoes, peeled and cut into chips
- 2 fish fillets of your choice
- 1 beaten egg
- 3 slices of wholemeal bread, grated into breadcrumbs
- 25g tortilla crisps
- 1 lemon rind and juice
- 1 tbsp parsley
- Salt and pepper to taste

Directions:

1. Preheat your air fryer to 200°C
2. Place the chips inside and cook until crispy
3. Cut the fish fillets into 4 slices and season with lemon juice
4. Place the breadcrumbs, lemon rind, parsley, tortillas and seasoning into a food processor and blitz to create a crumb consistency
5. Place the breadcrumbs on a large plate
6. Coat the fish in the egg and then the breadcrumb mixture
7. Cook for 15 minutes at 180°C

Pesto Salmon

Servings: 4
Cooking Time:xx

Ingredients:

- 4 x 150–175-g/5½–6-oz. salmon fillets
- lemon wedges, to serve
- PESTO
- 50 g/scant ½ cup toasted pine nuts
- 50 g/2 oz. fresh basil
- 50 g/⅔ cup grated Parmesan or Pecorino
- 100 ml/7 tablespoons olive oil

Directions:

1. To make the pesto, blitz the pine nuts, basil and Parmesan to a paste in a food processor. Pour in the olive oil and process again.
2. Preheat the air-fryer to 160°C/325°F.
3. Top each salmon fillet with 2 tablespoons of the pesto. Add the salmon fillets to the preheated air-fryer and air-fry for 9 minutes. Check the internal temperature of the fish has reached at least 63°C/145°F using a meat thermometer – if not, cook for another few minutes.

Garlic Tilapia

Servings: 2
Cooking Time:xx

Ingredients:

- 2 tilapia fillets
- 2 tsp chopped fresh chives
- 2 tsp chopped fresh parsley
- 2 tsp olive oil
- 1 tsp minced garlic
- Salt and pepper for seasoning

Directions:

1. Preheat the air fryer to 220°C
2. Take a small bowl and combine the olive oil with the chives, garlic, parsley and a little salt and pepper
3. Brush the mixture over the fish fillets
4. Place the fish into the air fryer and cook for 10 minutes, until flaky

Maine Seafood

Servings: 2
Cooking Time:xx

Ingredients:

- 500g flour
- 400g breadcrumbs
- 300g steamer clams
- 3 eggs
- 3 tbsp water

Directions:

1. Soak the clams for 3 hours, drain and rinse
2. Bring 1 inch of water to boil, add the clams and cover with a lid, steam for about 7 minutes until the clams open.
3. Remove the clams from the shell and set aside
4. Put the eggs in a bowl and mix with the water
5. Dip the clams in the flour, then the egg and then coat in breadcrumbs
6. Heat the air fryer to 180°C and cook for about 7 minutes

Fish Sticks With Tartar Sauce Batter

Servings: 4
Cooking Time:xx

Ingredients:

- 6 tbsp mayonnaise
- 2 tbsp dill pickle
- 1 tsp seafood seasoning
- 400g cod fillets, cut into sticks
- 300g panko breadcrumbs

Directions:

1. Combine the mayonnaise, seafood seasoning and dill pickle in a large bowl.
2. Add the cod sticks and coat well
3. Preheat air fryer to 200°C
4. Coat the fish sticks in the breadcrumbs
5. Place in the air fryer and cook for 12 minutes

Gluten Free Honey And Garlic Shrimp

Servings: 2
Cooking Time:xx

Ingredients:

- 500g fresh shrimp
- 5 tbsp honey
- 2 tbsp gluten free soy sauce
- 2 tbsp tomato ketchup
- 250g frozen stir fry vegetables
- 1 crushed garlic clove
- 1 tsp fresh ginger
- 2 tbsp cornstarch

Directions:

1. Simmer the honey, soy sauce, garlic, tomato ketchup and ginger in a saucepan
2. Add the cornstarch and whisk until sauce thickens
3. Coat the shrimp with the sauce
4. Line the air fryer with foil and add the shrimp and vegetables
5. Cook at 180°C for 10 minutes

Salt & Pepper Calamari

Servings: 2
Cooking Time:xx

Ingredients:

- 500g squid rings
- 500g panko breadcrumbs
- 250g plain flour
- 2 tbsp pepper
- 2 tbsp salt
- 200ml buttermilk
- 1 egg

Directions:

1. Take a medium bowl and combine the buttermilk and egg, stirring well
2. Take another bowl and combine the salt, pepper, flour, and panko breadcrumbs, combining again
3. Dip the quid into the buttermilk first and then the breadcrumbs, coating evenly
4. Place in the air fryer basket
5. Cook at 150°C for 12 minutes, until golden

Crispy Nacho Prawns

Servings: 6
Cooking Time:xx

Ingredients:

- 1 egg
- 18 large prawns
- 1 bag of nacho cheese flavoured corn chips, crushed

Directions:

1. Wash the prawns and pat dry
2. Place the chips into a bowl
3. In another bowl, whisk the egg
4. Dip the prawns into the egg and then the nachos
5. Preheat the air fryer to 180°C
6. Cook for 8 minutes

Cajun Shrimp Boil

Servings: 6

Cooking Time:xx

Ingredients:

- 300g cooked shrimp
- 14 slices of smoked sausage
- 5 par boiled potatoes, cut into halves
- 4 mini corn on the cobs, quartered
- 1 diced onion
- 3 tbsp old bay seasoning
- Olive oil spray

Directions:

1. Combine all the ingredients in a bowl and mix well
2. Line the air fryer with foil
3. Place half the mix into the air fryer and cook at 200°C for about 6 minutes, mix the ingredients and cook for a further 6 minutes.
4. Repeat for the second batch

Ranch Style Fish Fillets

Servings: 4

Cooking Time:xx

Ingredients:

- 200g bread crumbs
- 30g ranch-style dressing mix
- 2 tbsp oil
- 2 beaten eggs
- 4 fish fillets of your choice
- Lemon wedges to garnish

Directions:

1. Preheat air fryer to 180°C
2. Mix the bread crumbs and ranch dressing mix together, add in the oil until the mix becomes crumbly
3. Dip the fish into the, then cover in the breadcrumb mix
4. Place in the air fryer and cook for 12-13 minutes

Crunchy Fish

Servings: 4

Cooking Time:xx

Ingredients:

- 200g dry breadcrumbs
- 4 tbsp olive oil
- 4 fillets of white fish
- 1 beaten egg
- 1 sliced lemon

Directions:

1. Heat the fryer to 180°C
2. In a medium mixing bowl, combine the olive oil and the breadcrumbs
3. Take the fish and first dip it into the egg and then the breadcrumbs, making sure they are evenly coated well
4. Arrange the fish into the basket
5. Cook for 12 minutes
6. Remove and serve with lemon slices

Store-cupboard Fishcakes

Servings: 3
Cooking Time:xx

Ingredients:

- 400 g/14 oz. cooked potato – either mashed potato or the insides of jacket potatoes (see page 124)
- 2 x 150–200-g/5½–7-oz. cans fish, such as tuna or salmon, drained
- 2 eggs
- ¾ teaspoon salt
- 1 teaspoon dried parsley
- ½ teaspoon freshly ground black pepper
- 1 tablespoon olive oil
- caper dressing (see page 79), to serve

Directions:

1. Mix the cooked potato, fish, eggs, salt, parsley and pepper together in a bowl, then divide into 6 equal portions and form into fishcakes. Drizzle the olive oil over both sides of each fishcake.
2. Preheat the air-fryer to 180°C/350°F.
3. Add the fishcakes to the preheated air-fryer and air-fry for 15 minutes, turning halfway through cooking. Serve with salad and tartare sauce or Caper Dressing.

Cod Nuggets

Servings: 4
Cooking Time:xx

Ingredients:

- 400g cod fillets, cut into 8 chunks
- 35g flour
- 1 tbsp vegetable oil
- 200g cornflakes or cracker crumbs
- Egg wash - 1 tbsp egg and 1 tbsp water
- Salt and pepper to taste

Directions:

1. Crush the crackers or cornflakes to make crumbs, mix in the vegetable oil
2. Season the cod with salt and pepper and cover in flour, dip into the egg-wash then cover in crumbs
3. Set the air fryer to 180°C
4. Place the cod nuggets in the air fryer basket and cook for 15 minutes, until golden brown.

Garlic-parsley Prawns

Servings: 2
Cooking Time:xx

Ingredients:

- 300 g/10½ oz. raw king prawns/jumbo shrimp (without shell)
- 40 g/3 tablespoons garlic butter, softened (see page 72)
- 2 tablespoons freshly chopped flat-leaf parsley

Directions:

1. Thread the prawns/shrimp onto 6 metal skewers that will fit your air-fryer. Mix together the softened garlic butter and parsley and brush evenly onto the prawn skewers.
2. Preheat the air-fryer to 180°C/350°F.
3. Place the skewers on an air-fryer liner or a piece of pierced parchment paper. Add the skewers to the preheated air-fryer and air-fry for 2 minutes, then turn the skewers over and cook for a further 2 minutes. Check the internal temperature of the prawns has reached at least 50°C/120°F using a meat thermometer – if not, cook for another few minutes and serve.

Peppery Lemon Shrimp

Servings: 2
Cooking Time:xx
Ingredients:

- 300g uncooked shrimp
- 1 tbsp olive oil
- 1 the juice of 1 lemon
- 0.25 tsp garlic powder
- 1 sliced lemon
- 1 tsp pepper
- 0.25 tsp paprika

Directions:

1. Heat the fryer to 200°C
2. Take a medium sized mixing bowl and combine the lemon juice, pepper, garlic powder, paprika and the olive oil together
3. Add the shrimp to the bowl and make sure they're well coated
4. Arrange the shrimp into the basket of the fryer
5. Cook for between 6-8 minutes, until firm and pink

Poultry Recipes

Chicken And Wheat Stir Fry

Servings: 4
Cooking Time:xx
Ingredients:

- 1 onion
- 1 clove of garlic
- 200g skinless boneless chicken breast halves
- 3 whole tomatoes
- 400ml water
- 1 chicken stock cube
- 1 tbsp curry powder
- 130g wheat berries
- 1 tbsp vegetable oil

Directions:

1. Thinly slice the onion and garlic
2. Chop the chicken and tomatoes into cubes
3. Take a large saucepan and add the water, chicken stock, curry powder and wheat berries, combining well
4. Pour the oil into the air fryer bowl and heat for 5 minutes at 200°C
5. Add the remaining ingredients and pour the contents into the air fryer
6. Cook for 15 minutes

Hawaiian Chicken

Servings: 2
Cooking Time:xx

Ingredients:

- 2 chicken breasts
- 1 tbsp butter
- A pinch of salt and pepper
- 160ml pineapple juice
- 25g brown sugar
- 3 tbsp soy sauce
- 2 tsp water
- 1 clove of garlic, minced
- 1 tsp grated ginger
- 2 tsp cornstarch

Directions:

1. Preheat the air fryer to 260°C
2. Take a bowl and combine the butter and salt and pepper
3. Cover the chicken with the butter and cook in the fryer for 15 minutes, turning halfway
4. Remove and allow to rest for 5 minutes
5. Take another bowl and mix together the pineapple juice, soy sauce, garlic, ginger, and brown sugar
6. Transfer to a saucepan and simmer for 5 minutes
7. Combine the water and cornstarch and add to the sauce, stirring continually for another minute
8. Slice the chicken into strips and pour the sauce over the top

Garlic Parmesan Fried Chicken Wings

Servings: 4
Cooking Time:xx

Ingredients:

- 16 chicken wing drumettes
- Cooking spray
- 240ml low fat buttermilk
- 150g flour
- 140g grated parmesan
- 2 tbsp low sodium soy sauce
- 1 sachet of your favourite chicken seasoning
- 1 tsp garlic powder
- Salt and pepper to taste

Directions:

1. Place the chicken onto a cooking tray and pour the soy sauce over the top, ensuring it is fully coated
2. Season the chicken and place in the refrigerator for 30 minutes
3. Add the flour and parmesan into a ziplock bag
4. Coat the chicken with buttermilk and add it to the ziplock bag with the flour
5. Preheat your air fryer to 200°C
6. Place the chicken into the air fryer for 20 minutes
7. Shake the air fryer basket every 5 minutes until the 20 minutes is up

Grain-free Chicken Katsu

Servings: 4
Cooking Time:xx

Ingredients:

- 125 g/1¼ cups ground almonds
- ½ teaspoon salt
- ½ teaspoon garlic powder
- ½ teaspoon dried parsley
- ½ teaspoon freshly ground black pepper
- ¼ teaspoon onion powder
- ¼ teaspoon dried oregano
- 450 g/1 lb. mini chicken fillets
- 1 egg, beaten
- oil, for spraying/drizzling
- coriander/cilantro leaves, to serve
- KATSU SAUCE
- 1 teaspoon olive oil or avocado oil
- 1 courgette/zucchini (approx. 150 g/5 oz.), finely chopped
- 1 carrot (approx. 100 g/3½ oz.), finely chopped
- 1 onion (approx. 120 g/4½ oz.), finely chopped
- 1 eating apple (approx. 150 g/5 oz.), cored and finely chopped
- 1 teaspoon ground ginger
- 1 teaspoon ground turmeric
- 2 teaspoons ground cumin
- 2 teaspoons ground coriander
- 1½ teaspoons mild chilli/chili powder
- 1 teaspoon garlic powder
- 1½ tablespoons runny honey
- 1 tablespoon soy sauce (gluten-free if you wish)
- 700 ml/3 cups vegetable stock (700 ml/3 cups water with 1½ stock cubes)

Directions:

1. First make the sauce. The easiest way to ensure all the vegetables and apple are finely chopped is to combine them in a food processor. Heat the oil in a large saucepan and sauté the finely chopped vegetables and apple for 5 minutes. Add all the seasonings, honey, soy sauce and stock and stir well, then bring to a simmer and simmer for 30 minutes.
2. Meanwhile, mix together the ground almonds, seasonings and spices. Dip each chicken fillet into the beaten egg, then into the almond-spice mix, making sure each fillet is fully coated. Spray the coated chicken fillets with olive oil (or simply drizzle over).
3. Preheat the air-fryer to 180°C/350°F.
4. Place the chicken fillets in the preheated air-fryer and air-fry for 10 minutes, turning halfway through cooking. Check the internal temperature of the chicken has reached at least 74°C/165°F using a meat thermometer – if not, cook for another few minutes.
5. Blend the cooked sauce in a food processor until smooth. Serve the chicken with the Katsu Sauce drizzled over (if necessary, reheat the sauce gently before serving) and scattered with coriander leaves. Any unused sauce can be frozen.

Air Fried Maple Chicken Thighs

Servings: 4
Cooking Time:xx

Ingredients:

- 200ml buttermilk
- ½ tbsp maple syrup
- 1 egg
- 1 tsp granulated garlic salt
- 4 chicken thighs with the bone in
- 140g all purpose flour
- 65g tapioca flour
- 1 tsp sweet paprika
- 1 tsp onion powder
- ¼ tsp ground black pepper
- ¼ tsp cayenne pepper
- ½ tsp granulated garlic
- ½ tsp honey powder

Directions:

1. Take a bowl and combine the buttermilk, maple syrup, egg and garlic powder
2. Transfer to a bag and add chicken thighs, shaking to combine well
3. Set aside for 1 hour
4. Take a shallow bowl and add the flour, tapioca flour, salt, sweet paprika, smoked paprika, pepper, cayenne pepper and honey powder, combining well
5. Preheat the air fryer to 190°C
6. Drag the chicken through flour mixture and place the chicken skin side down in the air fryer Cook for 12 minutes, until white in the middle

Crunchy Chicken Tenders

Servings: 4
Cooking Time:xx

Ingredients:

- 8 regular chicken tenders (frozen work best)
- 1 egg
- 2 tbsp olive oil
- 150g dried breadcrumbs

Directions:

1. Heat the fryer to 175°C
2. In a small bowl, beat the egg
3. In another bowl, combine the oil and the breadcrumbs together
4. Take one tender and first dip it into the egg, and then cover it in the breadcrumb mixture
5. Place the tender into the fryer basket
6. Repeat with the rest of the tenders, arranging them carefully so they don't touch inside the basket
7. Cook for 12 minutes, checking that they are white in the centre before serving

Thai Turkey Burgers

Servings: 4
Cooking Time:xx

Ingredients:

- 1 courgette/zucchini, about 200 g/7 oz.
- 400 g/14 oz. minced/ground turkey breast
- 35 g/½ cup fresh breadcrumbs (gluten-free if you wish)
- 1 teaspoon Thai 7 spice seasoning
- 1 teaspoon salt
- 1 teaspoon olive oil

Directions:

1. Coarsely grate the courgette/zucchini, then place in a piece of muslin/cheesecloth and squeeze out the water. Combine the grated courgette with all other ingredients except the olive oil, mixing together well. Divide the mixture into 4 equal portions and mould into burgers. Brush with oil.
2. Preheat the air-fryer to 190°C/375°C.
3. Add the turkey burgers to the preheated air-fryer and air-fry for 15 minutes, turning once halfway through cooking. Check the internal temperature of the burgers has reached at least 74°C/165°F using a meat thermometer – if not, cook for another few minutes and then serve.

Chicken Tikka

Servings: 2
Cooking Time:xx

Ingredients:

- 2 chicken breasts, diced
- FIRST MARINADE
- freshly squeezed juice of ½ a lemon
- 1 tablespoon freshly grated ginger
- 1 tablespoon freshly grated garlic
- a good pinch of salt
- SECOND MARINADE
- 100 g/½ cup Greek yogurt
- ½ teaspoon chilli powder
- ½ teaspoon chilli paste
- ½ teaspoon turmeric
- ½ teaspoon garam masala
- 1 tablespoon olive oil

Directions:

1. Mix the ingredients for the first marinade together in a bowl, add in the chicken and stir to coat all the chicken pieces. Leave in the fridge to marinate for 20 minutes.
2. Combine the second marinade ingredients. Once the first marinade has had 20 minutes, add the second marinade to the chicken and stir well. Leave in the fridge for at least 4 hours.
3. Preheat the air-fryer to 180°C/350°F.
4. Thread the chicken pieces onto metal skewers that fit in your air-fryer. Add the skewers to the preheated air-fryer and air-fry for 10 minutes. Check the internal temperature of the chicken has reached at least 74°C/165°F using a meat thermometer – if not, cook for another few minutes and then serve.

Pizza Chicken Nuggets

Servings: 2

Cooking Time:xx

Ingredients:

- 60 g/¾ cup dried breadcrumbs (see page 9)
- 20 g/¼ cup grated Parmesan
- ½ teaspoon dried oregano
- ¼ teaspoon freshly ground black pepper
- 150 g/⅔ cup Mediterranean sauce (see page 102) or 150 g/5½ oz. jarred tomato pasta sauce (keep any leftover sauce for serving)
- 400 g/14 oz. chicken fillets

Directions:

1. Preheat the air-fryer to 180°C/350°F.
2. Combine the breadcrumbs, Parmesan, oregano and pepper in a bowl. Have the Mediterranean or pasta sauce in a separate bowl.
3. Dip each chicken fillet in the tomato sauce first, then roll in the breadcrumb mix until coated fully.
4. Add the breaded fillets to the preheated air-fryer and air-fry for 10 minutes. Check the internal temperature of the chicken has reached at least 74°C/165°F using a meat thermometer – if not, cook for another few minutes.
5. Serve with some additional sauce that has been warmed through.

Cornflake Chicken Nuggets

Servings: 4

Cooking Time:xx

Ingredients:

- 100 g/4 cups cornflakes (gluten-free if you wish)
- 70 g/½ cup plus ½ tablespoon plain/all-purpose flour (gluten-free if you wish)
- 2 eggs, beaten
- ½ teaspoon salt
- ¼ teaspoon freshly ground black pepper
- 600 g/1 lb. 5 oz. mini chicken fillets

Directions:

1. Grind the cornflakes in a food processor to a crumb-like texture. Place the flour in one bowl and the beaten eggs in a second bowl; season both bowls with the salt and pepper. Coat each chicken fillet in flour, tapping off any excess. Next dip each flour-coated chicken fillet into the egg, then the cornflakes until fully coated.
2. Preheat the air-fryer to 180°C/350°F.
3. Add the chicken fillets to the preheated air-fryer (you may need to add the fillets in two batches, depending on the size of your air-fryer) and air-fry for 10 minutes, turning halfway through cooking. Check the internal temperature of the nuggets has reached at least 74°C/165°F using a meat thermometer – if not, cook for another few minutes and then serve.
4. VARIATION: SIMPLE CHICKEN NUGGETS
5. For a simpler version, replace the crushed cornflakes with 90 g/1¼ cups dried breadcrumbs (see page 9). Prepare and air-fry in the same way.

Chicken Fried Rice

Servings: 4
Cooking Time:xx

Ingredients:

- 400g cooked white rice
- 400g cooked chicken, diced
- 200g frozen peas and carrots
- 6 tbsp soy sauce
- 1 tbsp vegetable oil
- 1 diced onion

Directions:

1. Take a large bowl and add the rice, vegetable oil and soy sauce and combine well
2. Add the frozen peas, carrots, diced onion and the chicken and mix together well
3. Pour the mixture into a nonstick pan
4. Place the pan into the air fryer
5. Cook at 182C for 20 minutes

Nashville Chicken

Servings: 4
Cooking Time:xx

Ingredients:

- 400g boneless chicken breast tenders
- 2 tsp salt
- 2 tsp coarsely ground black pepper
- 2 tbsp hot sauce
- 2 tbsp pickle juice
- 500g all purpose flour
- 3 large eggs
- 300ml buttermilk
- 2 tbsp olive oil
- 6 tbsp cayenne pepper
- 3 tbsp dark brown sugar
- 1 tsp chilli powder
- 1 tsp garlic powder
- 1 tsp paprika
- Salt and pepper to taste

Directions:

1. Take a large mixing bowl and add the chicken, hot sauce, pickle juice, salt and pepper and combine
2. Place in the refrigerator for 3 hours
3. Transfer the flour to a bowl
4. Take another bowl and add the eggs, buttermilk and 1 tbsp of the hot sauce, combining well
5. Press each piece of chicken into the flour and coat well
6. Place the chicken into the buttermilk mixture and then back into the flour
7. Allow to sit or 10 minutes
8. Preheat the air fryer to 193C
9. Whisk together the spices, brown sugar and olive oil to make the sauce and pour over the chicken tenders
10. Serve whilst still warm

Chicken And Cheese Chimichangas

Servings: 6
Cooking Time:xx

Ingredients:

- 100g shredded chicken (cooked)
- 150g nacho cheese
- 1 chopped jalapeño pepper
- 6 flour tortillas
- 5 tbsp salsa
- 60g refried beans
- 1 tsp cumin
- 0.5 tsp chill powder
- Salt and pepper to taste

Directions:

1. Take a large mixing bowl and add all of the ingredients, combining well
2. Add ⅓ of the filling to each tortilla and roll into a burrito shape
3. Spray the air fryer with cooking spray and heat to 200°C
4. Place the chimichangas in the air fryer and cook for 7 minutes

Chicken Fajitas

Servings: 3
Cooking Time:xx

Ingredients:

- 2 boneless chicken breasts, sliced into strips
- 5 mini (bell) peppers, sliced into strips
- 1 courgette/zucchini, sliced into 5-mm/¼-in. thick discs
- 2 tablespoons olive oil
- 28-g/1-oz. packet fajita seasoning mix
- TO SERVE
- wraps
- sliced avocado
- chopped tomato and red onion
- grated Red Leicester cheese
- plain yogurt
- coriander/cilantro
- lime wedges, for squeezing

Directions:

1. Combine the chicken, (bell) peppers, courgettes/zucchini and olive oil in a bowl. Add the fajita seasoning and stir to coat.
2. Preheat the air-fryer to 180°C/350°F.
3. Add the coated vegetables and chicken to the preheated air-fryer and air-fry for 12 minutes, shaking the drawer a couple of times during cooking. Check the internal temperature of the chicken has reached at least 74°C/165°F using a meat thermometer – if not, cook for another few minutes.
4. Serve immediately alongside the serving suggestions or your own choices of accompaniments.

Chicken Milanese

Servings: 4
Cooking Time:xx

Ingredients:

- 130 g/1¾ cups dried breadcrumbs (gluten-free if you wish, see page 9)
- 50 g/⅔ cup grated Parmesan
- 1 teaspoon dried basil
- ½ teaspoon dried thyme
- ¼ teaspoon freshly ground black pepper
- 1 egg, beaten
- 4 tablespoons plain/all-purpose flour (gluten-free if you wish)
- 4 boneless chicken breasts

Directions:

1. Combine the breadcrumbs, cheese, herbs and pepper in a bowl. In a second bowl beat the egg, and in the third bowl have the plain/all-purpose flour. Dip each chicken breast first into the flour, then the egg, then the seasoned breadcrumbs.
2. Preheat the air-fryer to 180°C/350°F.
3. Add the breaded chicken breasts to the preheated air-fryer and air-fry for 12 minutes. Check the internal temperature of the chicken has reached at least 74°C/165°F using a meat thermometer – if not, cook for another few minutes.

Quick Chicken Nuggets

Servings: 4
Cooking Time:xx

Ingredients:

- 500g chicken tenders
- 25g ranch salad dressing mixture
- 2 tbsp plain flour
- 100g breadcrumbs
- 1 egg, beaten
- Olive oil spray

Directions:

1. Take a large mixing bowl and arrange the chicken inside
2. Sprinkle the seasoning over the top and ensure the chicken is evenly coated
3. Place the chicken to one side for around 10 minutes
4. Add the flour into a resealable bag
5. Crack the egg into a small mixing bowl and whisk
6. Pour the breadcrumbs onto a medium sized plate
7. Transfer the chicken into the resealable bag and coat with the flour, giving it a good shake
8. Remove the chicken and dip into the egg, and then rolling it into the breadcrumbs, coating evenly
9. Repeat with all pieces of the chicken
10. Heat your air fryer to 200°C
11. Arrange the chicken inside the fryer and add a little olive oil spray to avoid sticking
12. Cook for 4 minutes, before turning over and cooking for another 4 minutes
13. Remove and serve whilst hot

Chicken Jalfrezi

Servings: 4
Cooking Time:xx

Ingredients:

- 500g chicken breasts
- 1 tbsp water
- 4 tbsp tomato sauce
- 1 chopped onion
- 1 chopped bell pepper
- 2 tsp love oil
- 1 tsp turmeric
- 1 tsp cayenne pepper
- 2 tsp garam masala
- Salt and pepper to taste

Directions:

1. Take a large mixing bowl and add the chicken, onions, pepper, salt, garam masala, turmeric, oil and cayenne pepper, combining well
2. Place the chicken mix in the air fryer and cook at 180°C for 15 minutes
3. Take a microwave-safe bowl and add the tomato sauce, water salt, garam masala and cayenne, combining well
4. Cook in the microwave for 1 minute, stir then cook for a further minute
5. Remove the chicken from the air fryer and pour the sauce over the top.
6. Serve whilst still warm

Air Fryer Chicken Thigh Schnitzel

Servings: 4
Cooking Time:xx

Ingredients:

- 300g boneless chicken thighs
- 160g seasoned breadcrumbs
- 1 tsp salt
- ½ tsp ground black pepper
- 30g flour
- 1 egg
- Cooking spray

Directions:

1. Lay the chicken on a sheet of parchment paper and add another on top
2. Use a mallet or a rolling pin to flatten it down
3. Take a bowl and add the breadcrumbs with the salt and pepper
4. Place the flour into another bowl
5. Dip the chicken into the flour, then the egg, and then the breadcrumbs
6. Preheat air fryer to 190°C
7. Place the chicken into the air fryer and spray with cooking oil
8. Cook for 6 minutes

Whole Chicken

Servings: 4

Cooking Time:xx

Ingredients:

- 1.5-kg/3¼-lb. chicken
- 2 tablespoons butter or coconut oil
- salt and freshly ground black pepper

Directions:

1. Place the chicken breast-side up and carefully insert the butter or oil between the skin and the flesh of each breast. Season.
2. Preheat the air-fryer to 180°C/350°F. If the chicken hits the heating element, remove the drawer to lower the chicken a level.
3. Add the chicken to the preheated air-fryer breast-side up. Air-fry for 30 minutes, then turn over and cook for a further 10 minutes. Check the internal temperature with a meat thermometer. If it is 75°C/167°F at the thickest part, remove the chicken from the air-fryer and leave to rest for 10 minutes before carving. If less than 75°C/167°F, continue to cook until this internal temperature is reached and then allow to rest.

Orange Chicken

Servings: 2

Cooking Time:xx

Ingredients:

- 600g chicken thighs, boneless and skinless
- 2 tbsp cornstarch
- 60ml orange juice
- 1 tbsp soy sauce
- 2 tbsp brown sugar
- 1 tbsp rice wine vinegar
- 1/4 teaspoon ground ginger
- Pinch of red pepper flakes
- Zest of one orange
- 2 tsp water and 2 tsp cornstarch mixed together

Directions:

1. Preheat your air fryer to 250°C
2. Take a bowl and combine the chicken with the cornstarch
3. Place in the air fryer and cook for 9 minutes
4. Take a bowl and combine the rest of the ingredients, except for the water and cornstarch mixture
5. Place in a saucepan and bring to the boil and then turn down to a simmer for 5 minutes
6. Add the water and cornstarch mixture to the pan and combine well
7. Remove the chicken from the fryer and pour the sauce over the top

Bbq Chicken Tenders

Servings: 6

Cooking Time:xx

Ingredients:

- 300g barbecue flavoured pork rinds
- 200g all purpose flour
- 1 tbsp barbecue seasoning
- 1 egg
- 400g chicken breast tenderloins

- Cooking spray

Directions:

1. Preheat the air fryer to 190°C
2. Place the pork rinds into a food processor and blitz to a breadcrumb consistency, before transferring to a bowl
3. In a separate bowl, combine the flour and barbecue seasoning
4. Beat the egg in a small bowl
5. Take the chicken and first dip into the egg, then the flour, and then the breadcrumbs
6. Place the chicken into the air fryer and spray with cooking spray and cook for about 15 minutes

Crispy Cornish Hen

Servings: 4

Cooking Time:xx

Ingredients:

- 2 Cornish hens, weighing around 500g each
- 2 tbsp olive oil
- 1 tsp garlic powder
- 1 tsp paprika
- 1.5 tsp Italian seasoning
- 1 tbsp lemon juice
- Salt and pepper to taste

Directions:

1. Preheat your air fryer to 260°C
2. Combine all the ingredients into a bowl (except for the hens) until smooth
3. Brush the hens with the mixture, coating evenly
4. Place in the air fryer basket, with the breast side facing down
5. Cook for 35 minutes
6. Turn over and cook for another 10 minutes
7. Ensure the hens are white in the middle before serving

Air Fryer Sesame Chicken Thighs

Servings: 4

Cooking Time:xx

Ingredients:

- 2 tbsp sesame oil
- 2 tbsp soy sauce
- 1 tbsp honey
- 1 tbsp sriracha sauce
- 1 tsp rice vinegar
- 400g chicken thighs
- 1 green onion, chopped
- 2 tbsp toasted sesame seeds

Directions:

1. Take a large bowl and combine the sesame oil, soy sauce, honey, sriracha and vinegar
2. Add the chicken and refrigerate for 30 minutes
3. Preheat the air fryer to 200°C
4. Cook for 5 minutes
5. Flip and then cook for another 10 minutes
6. Serve with green onion and sesame seeds

Side Dishes Recipes

Sweet And Sticky Parsnips And Carrots

Servings:2
Cooking Time:15 Minutes
Ingredients:

- 4 large carrots, peeled and chopped into long chunks
- 4 large parsnips, peeled and chopped into long chunks
- 1 tbsp olive oil
- 2 tbsp honey
- 1 tsp dried mixed herbs

Directions:

1. Preheat the air fryer to 150 °C / 300 °F and line the bottom of the basket with parchment paper.
2. Place the chopped carrots and parsnips in a large bowl and drizzle over the olive oil and honey. Sprinkle in some black pepper to taste and toss well to fully coat the vegetables.
3. Transfer the coated vegetables into the air fryer basket and shut the lid. Cook for 20 minutes until the carrots and parsnips and cooked and crispy.
4. Serve as a side with your dinner.

Ricotta Stuffed Aubergine

Servings: 2
Cooking Time:xx
Ingredients:

- 1 aubergine
- 150g ricotta cheese
- 75g Parmesan cheese, plus an extra 75g for the breading
- 1 tsp garlic powder
- 3 tbsp parsley
- 1 egg, plus an extra 2 eggs for the breading
- 300g pork rind crumbs
- 2 tsp Italian seasoning

Directions:

1. Cut the aubergine into rounds, about 1/2" in thickness
2. Line a baking sheet with parchment and arrange the rounds on top, sprinkling with salt
3. Place another sheet of parchment on top and place something heavy on top to get rid of excess water
4. Leave for 30 minutes
5. Take a bowl and combine the egg, ricotta, 75g Parmesan and parsley, until smooth
6. Remove the parchment from the aubergine and wipe off the salt
7. Take a tablespoon of the ricotta mixture and place on top of each round of aubergine, spreading with a knife
8. Place in the freezer for a while to set
9. Take a bowl and add the two eggs, the pork rinds, parmesan and seasonings, and combine
10. Remove the aubergine from the freezer and coat each one in the mixture completely
11. Place back in the freezer for 45 minutes
12. Cook in the air fryer for 8 minutes at 250°C

Garlic And Parsley Potatoes

Servings: 4
Cooking Time:xx

Ingredients:

- 500g baby potatoes, cut into quarters
- 1 tbsp oil
- 1 tsp salt
- ½ tsp garlic powder
- ½ tsp dried parsley

Directions:

1. Preheat air fryer to 175°C
2. Combine potatoes and oil in a bowl
3. Add remaining ingredients and mix
4. Add to the air fryer and cook for about 25 minutes until golden brown, turning halfway through

Potato Wedges

Servings: 4
Cooking Time:xx

Ingredients:

- 2 potatoes, cut into wedges
- 1 ½ tbsp olive oil
- ½ tsp paprika
- ⅛ tsp ground black pepper
- ½ tsp parsley flakes
- ½ tsp chilli powder
- ½ tsp sea salt

Directions:

1. Preheat the air fryer to 200°C
2. Add all ingredients to a bowl and combine well
3. Place the wedges into the air fryer and cook for 10 minutes
4. Turn and cook for a further 8 minutes until golden brown

Crispy Sweet & Spicy Cauliflower

Servings: 2
Cooking Time:xx

Ingredients:

- ½ a head of cauliflower
- 1 teaspoon sriracha sauce
- 1 teaspoon soy sauce (or tamari)
- ½ teaspoon maple syrup
- 2 teaspoons olive oil or avocado oil

Directions:

1. Preheat the air-fryer to 180°C/350°F.
2. Chop the cauliflower into florets with a head size of roughly 5 cm/1 in. Place the other ingredients in a bowl and mix together, then add the florets and toss to coat them.
3. Add the cauliflower to the preheated air-fryer and air-fry for 12 minutes, shaking the drawer a couple of times during cooking.

Spicy Green Beans

Servings: 4
Cooking Time:xx

Ingredients:

- 300g green beans
- 1 tbsp sesame oil
- 1 tsp soy
- 1 tsp rice wine vinegar
- 1 clove garlic, minced
- 1 tsp red pepper flakes

Directions:

1. Preheat air fryer to 200°C
2. Place green beans in a bowl
3. Mix together remaining ingredients, add green beans and fully coat
4. Place in the air fryer and cook for 12 minutes

Egg Fried Rice

Servings:2
Cooking Time:15 Minutes

Ingredients:

- 400 g / 14 oz cooked white or brown rice
- 100 g / 3.5 oz fresh peas and sweetcorn
- 2 tbsp olive oil
- 2 eggs, scrambled

Directions:

1. Preheat the air fryer to 150 °C / 300 °F and line the bottom of the basket with parchment paper.
2. In a bowl, mix the cooked white or brown rice and the fresh peas and sweetcorn.
3. Pour in 2 tbsp olive oil and toss to coat evenly. Stir in the scrambled eggs.
4. Transfer the egg rice into the lined air fryer basket, close the lid, and cook for 15 minutes until the eggs are cooked and the rice is soft.
5. Serve as a side dish with some cooked meat or tofu.

Shishito Peppers

Servings: 2
Cooking Time:xx

Ingredients:

- 200g shishito peppers
- Salt and pepper to taste
- ½ tbsp avocado oil
- 75g grated cheese
- 2 limes

Directions:

1. Rinse the peppers
2. Place in a bowl and mix with oil, salt and pepper
3. Place in the air fryer and cook at 175°C for 10 minutes
4. Place on a serving plate and sprinkle with cheese

Mexican Rice

Servings: 4
Cooking Time:xx
Ingredients:

- 500g long grain rice
- 3 tbsp olive oil
- 60ml water
- 1 tsp chilli powder
- 1/4 tsp cumin
- 2 tbsp tomato paste
- 1/2 tsp garlic powder
- 1tsp red pepper flakes
- 1 chopped onion
- 500ml chicken stock
- Half a small jalapeño pepper with seeds out, chopped
- Salt for seasoning

Directions:

1. Add the water and tomato paste and combine, placing to one side
2. Take a baking pan and add a little oil
3. Wash the rice and add to the baking pan
4. Add the chicken stock, tomato paste, jalapeños, onions, and the rest of the olive oil, and combine
5. Place aluminium foil over the top and place in your air fryer
6. Cook at 220°C for 50 minutes
7. Keep checking the rice as it cooks, as the liquid should be absorbing

Homemade Croquettes

Servings:4
Cooking Time:15 Minutes
Ingredients:

- 400 g / 14 oz white rice, uncooked
- 1 onion, sliced
- 2 cloves garlic, finely sliced
- 2 eggs, beaten
- 50 g / 3.5 oz parmesan cheese, grated
- 1 tsp salt
- 1 tsp black pepper
- 50 g / 3.5 oz breadcrumbs
- 1 tsp dried oregano

Directions:

1. In a large mixing bowl, combine the white rice, onion slices, garlic cloves slices, one beaten egg, parmesan cheese, and a sprinkle of salt and pepper.
2. Whisk the second egg in a separate bowl and place the breadcrumbs into another bowl.
3. Shape the mixture into 12 even croquettes and roll evenly in the egg, followed by the breadcrumbs.
4. Preheat the air fryer to 190 °C / 375 °F and line the bottom of the basket with parchment paper.
5. Place the croquettes in the lined air fryer basket and cook for 15 minutes, turning halfway through, until crispy and golden. Enjoy while hot as a side to your main dish.

Zingy Roasted Carrots

Servings: 4
Cooking Time:xx
Ingredients:

- 500g carrots
- 1 tsp olive oil
- 1 tsp cayenne pepper
- Salt and pepper for seasoning

Directions:

1. Peel the carrots and cut them into chunks, around 2" in size
2. Preheat your air fryer to 220°C
3. Add the carrots to a bowl with the olive oil and cayenne and toss to coat
4. Place in the fryer and cook for 15 minutes, giving them a stir halfway through
5. Season before serving

Cauliflower With Hot Sauce And Blue Cheese Sauce

Servings:2
Cooking Time:15 Minutes
Ingredients:

- For the cauliflower:
- 1 cauliflower, broken into florets
- 4 tbsp hot sauce
- 2 tbsp olive oil
- 1 tsp garlic powder
- ½ tsp salt
- ½ tsp black pepper
- 1 tbsp plain flour
- 1 tbsp corn starch
- For the blue cheese sauce:
- 50 g / 1.8 oz blue cheese, crumbled
- 2 tbsp sour cream
- 2 tbsp mayonnaise
- ½ tsp salt
- ½ tsp black pepper

Directions:

1. Preheat the air fryer to 180 °C / 350 °F and line the bottom of the basket with parchment paper.
2. In a bowl, combine the hot sauce, olive oil, garlic powder, salt, and black pepper until it forms a consistent mixture. Add the cauliflower to the bowl and coat in the sauce.
3. Stir in the plain flour and corn starch until well combined.
4. Transfer the cauliflower to the lined basket in the air fryer, close the lid, and cook for 12-15 minutes until the cauliflower has softened and is golden in colour.
5. Meanwhile, make the blue cheese sauce by combining all of the ingredients. When the cauliflower is ready, remove it from the air fryer and serve with the blue cheese sauce on the side.

Celery Root Fries

Servings: 2
Cooking Time:xx

Ingredients:

- ½ celeriac, cut into sticks
- 500ml water
- 1 tbsp lime juice
- 1 tbsp olive oil
- 75g mayo
- 1 tbsp mustard
- 1 tbsp powdered horseradish

Directions:

1. Put celeriac in a bowl, add water and lime juice, soak for 30 minutes
2. Preheat air fryer to 200
3. Mix together the mayo, horseradish powder and mustard, refrigerate
4. Drain the celeriac, drizzle with oil and season with salt and pepper
5. Place in the air fryer and cook for about 10 minutes turning halfway
6. Serve with the mayo mix as a dip

Butternut Squash Fries

Servings: 4
Cooking Time:xx

Ingredients:

- 400g butternut squash, cut into sticks
- 1 tbsp olive oil
- 2 tbsp bagel seasoning
- 1 tsp fresh chopped rosemary

Directions:

1. Preheat air fryer to 200°C
2. Drizzle butternut squash with olive oil mix to coat
3. Add to the air fryer, cook for about 22 minutes until golden brown, stirring every 4 minutes
4. Sprinkle with bagel seasoning to serve

Sweet Potato Tots

Servings: 24
Cooking Time:xx

Ingredients:

- 2 sweet potatoes, peeled
- ½ tsp cajun seasoning
- Olive oil cooking spray
- Sea salt to taste

Directions:

1. Boil the sweet potatoes in a pan for about 15 minutes, allow to cool
2. Grate the sweet potato and mix in the cajun seasoning
3. Form into tot shaped cylinders
4. Spray the air fryer with oil, place the tots in the air fryer
5. Sprinkle with salt and cook for 8 minutes at 200°C, turn and cook for another 8 minutes

Zingy Brussels Sprouts

Servings: 2
Cooking Time:xx

Ingredients:

- 1 tbsp avocado oil
- ½ tsp salt
- ½ tsp pepper
- 400g Brussels sprouts halved
- 1 tsp balsamic vinegar
- 2 tsp crumbled bacon

Directions:

1. Preheat air fryer to 175°C
2. Combine oil, salt and pepper in a bowl and mix well. Add Brussels sprouts
3. Place in the air fryer and cook for 5 minutes shake then cook for another 5 minutes
4. Sprinkle with balsamic vinegar and sprinkle with bacon

Potato Wedges With Rosemary

Servings: 2
Cooking Time:xx

Ingredients:

- 2 potatoes, sliced into wedges
- 1 tbsp olive oil
- 2 tsp seasoned salt
- 2 tbsp chopped rosemary

Directions:

1. Preheat air fryer to 190°C
2. Drizzle potatoes with oil, mix in salt and rosemary
3. Place in the air fryer and cook for 20 minutes turning halfway

Butternut Squash

Servings: 4
Cooking Time:xx

Ingredients:

- 500 g/1 lb. 2 oz. butternut squash, chopped into 2.5-cm/1-in. cubes
- 1 tablespoon olive oil or avocado oil
- 1 teaspoon smoked paprika
- 1 teaspoon dried oregano
- ½ teaspoon salt
- ¼ teaspoon freshly ground black pepper

Directions:

1. Preheat the air-fryer to 180°C/350°F.
2. In a bowl toss the butternut squash cubes in the oil and all the seasonings.
3. Add the butternut squash cubes to the preheated air-fryer and air-fry for 16–18 minutes, shaking the drawer once during cooking.

Orange Tofu

Servings: 4
Cooking Time:xx
Ingredients:

- 400g tofu, drained
- 1 tbsp tamari
- 1 tbsp corn starch
- ¼ tsp pepper flakes
- 1 tsp minced ginger
- 1 tsp fresh garlic
- 1 tsp orange zest
- 75ml orange juice
- 75ml water
- 2 tsp cornstarch
- 1 tbsp maple syrup

Directions:

1. Cut the tofu into cubes, place in a bowl add the tamari and mix well
2. Mix in 1 tbsp starch and allow to marinate for 30 minutes
3. Place the remaining ingredients into another bowl and mix well
4. Place the tofu in the air fryer and cook at 190°C for about 10 minutes
5. Add tofu to a pan with sauce mix and cook until sauce thickens

Crispy Cinnamon French Toast

Servings:2
Cooking Time:5 Minutes
Ingredients:

- 4 slices white bread
- 4 eggs
- 200 ml milk (cow's milk, cashew milk, soy milk, or oat milk)
- 2 tbsp granulated sugar
- 1 tsp brown sugar
- 1 tsp vanilla extract
- ½ tsp ground cinnamon

Directions:

1. Preheat your air fryer to 150 °C / 300 °F and line the bottom of the basket with parchment paper.
2. Cut each of the bread slices into 2 even rectangles and set them aside.
3. In a mixing bowl, whisk together the 4 eggs, milk, granulated sugar, brown sugar, vanilla extract, and ground cinnamon.
4. Soak the bread pieces in the egg mixture until they are fully covered and soaked in the mixture.
5. Place the coated bread slices in the lined air fryer, close the lid, and cook for 4-5 minutes until the bread is crispy and golden.
6. Serve the French toast slices with whatever toppings you desire.

Courgette Gratin

Servings: 2
Cooking Time:xx
Ingredients:

- 2 courgette
- 1 tbsp chopped parsley
- 2 tbsp breadcrumbs
- 4 tbsp grated parmesan
- 1 tbsp vegetable oil
- Salt and pepper to taste

Directions:

1. Heat the air fryer to 180°C
2. Cut each courgette in half length ways then slice
3. Mix the remaining ingredients together
4. Place the courgette in the air fryer and top with the breadcrumb mix
5. Cook for about 15 minutes until golden brown

Corn On The Cob

Servings: 4
Cooking Time:xx
Ingredients:

- 75g mayo
- 2 tsp grated cheese
- 1 tsp lime juice
- ¼ tsp chilli powder
- 2 ears of corn, cut into 4

Directions:

1. Heat the air fryer to 200°C
2. Mix the mayo, cheese lime juice and chilli powder in a bowl
3. Cover the corn in the mayo mix
4. Place in the air fryer and cook for 8 minutes

Hasselback New Potatoes

Servings: 4
Cooking Time:xx
Ingredients:

- 8–12 new potatoes, roughly 5–7 cm/2–2¾ in. in length
- 2 teaspoons olive oil
- salt
- 1 tablespoon butter (optional)

Directions:

1. Preheat the air-fryer to 180°C/350°F.
2. Slice the potatoes multiple times widthways, making sure you do not cut all the way through (if you place the potatoes in the bowl of a wooden spoon to make these slices, it prevents you cutting all the way through). Coat the potatoes in the olive oil and sprinkle over the salt.
3. Add the potatoes to the preheated air-fryer and air-fry for 20–25 minutes until the potatoes are crispy on the outside but soft on the inside. Serve immediately.

Chocolate Orange Muffins

Servings: 12
Cooking Time:xx

Ingredients:

- 100g self raising flour
- 110g caster sugar
- 50g butter
- 20g cocoa powder
- 50ml milk
- 1 tsp cocoa nibs
- 1 large orange juice and rind
- 1 tbsp honey
- 1tsp vanilla essence
- 2 eggs

Directions:

1. Add the flour, butter and sugar to a mixing bowl and rug together
2. Add the cocoa, honey, orange and vanilla mix well
3. Mix the milk and egg together then add to the flour mix, combine well
4. Rub your muffin cases with flour to stop them sticking, add 2 tbsp batter to each one
5. Cook in the air fryer for 12 minutes at 180°C

Mini Egg Buns

Servings: 8
Cooking Time:xx

Ingredients:

- 100g self raising flour
- 100g caster sugar
- 100g butter
- 2 eggs
- 2 tbsp honey
- 1 tbsp vanilla essence
- 300g soft cheese
- 100g icing sugar
- 2 packets of Mini Eggs

Directions:

1. Cream the butter and sugar together until light and fluffy, beat in the eggs one at a time
2. Add the honey and vanilla essence, fold in the flour a bit at a time
3. Divide the mix into 8 bun cases and place in the air fryer. Cook at 180°C for about 20 minutes
4. Cream the soft cheese and icing sugar together to make the topping
5. Allow the buns to cool, pipe on the topping mix and add mini eggs

Shortbread Cookies

Servings: 2
Cooking Time:xx
Ingredients:

- 250g flour
- 75g sugar
- 175g butter
- 1 tbsp vanilla essence
- Chocolate buttons for decoration

Directions:

1. Preheat air fryer to 180°C
2. Place all ingredients apart from the chocolate into a bowl and rub together
3. Form into dough and roll out. Cut into heart shapes using a cookie cutter
4. Place in the air fryer and cook for 10 minutes
5. Place the chocolate buttons onto the shortbread and cook for another 10 minutes at 160°C

Strawberry Lemonade Pop Tarts

Servings: 12
Cooking Time:xx
Ingredients:

- 300g whole wheat flour
- 225g white flour
- ¼ tsp salt
- 2 tbsp light brown sugar
- 300g icing sugar
- 2 tbsp lemon juice
- Zest of 1 lemon
- 150g cold coconut oil
- 1 tsp vanilla extract
- 75ml ice cold water
- Strawberry Jam
- 1 tsp melted coconut oil
- ¼ tsp vanilla extract
- Sprinkles

Directions:

1. In a bowl mix the flours, salt and sugar. Mix in the cold coconut oil
2. Add 1 tsp vanilla and 1 tbsp at a time of the ice cold water, mix until a dough is formed
3. Take the dough and roll out thinly on a floured surface. Cut into 5cm by 7cm rectangles
4. Place a tsp of jam in the centre of half the rectangles, wet the edges place another rectangle on the top and seal
5. Place in the air fryer and cook at 200°C for 10 minutes. Allow to cool
6. Mix the icing sugar, coconut oil, lemon juice and lemon zest in a bowl. Mix well. Top the pop tarts and add sprinkles to serve

Apple Crumble

Servings: 4
Cooking Time:xx

Ingredients:

- 2 apples (each roughly 175 g/6 oz.), cored and chopped into 2-cm/¾-in cubes
- 3 tablespoons unrefined sugar
- 100 g/1 cup jumbo rolled oats/old-fashioned oats
- 40 g/heaped ¼ cup flour (gluten-free if you wish)
- 1 heaped teaspoon ground cinnamon
- 70 g/scant ⅓ cup cold butter, chopped into small cubes

Directions:

1. Preheat the air-fryer to 180°C/350°F.
2. Scatter the apple pieces in a baking dish that fits your air-fryer, then sprinkle over 1 tablespoon sugar. Add the baking dish to the preheated air-fryer and air-fry for 5 minutes.
3. Meanwhile, in a bowl mix together the oats, flour, remaining sugar and cold butter. Use your fingertips to bring the crumble topping together.
4. Remove the baking dish from the air-fryer and spoon the crumble topping over the partially cooked apple. Return the baking dish to the air dryer and air-fry for a further 10 minutes. Serve warm or cold.

Thai Fried Bananas

Servings: 8
Cooking Time:xx

Ingredients:

- 4 ripe bananas
- 2 tbsp flour
- 2 tbsp rice flour
- 2 tbsp cornflour
- 2 tbsp desiccated coconut
- Pinch salt
- ½ tsp baking powder
- ½ tsp cardamon powder

Directions:

1. Place all the dry ingredients in a bowl and mix well. Add a little water at a time and combine to form a batter
2. Cut the bananas in half and then half again length wise
3. Line the air fryer with parchment paper and spray with cooking spray
4. Dip each banana piece in the batter mix and place in the air fryer
5. Cook at 200°C for 10 -15 minutes turning halfway
6. Serve with ice cream

Fried Oreos

Servings: 8
Cooking Time:xx

Ingredients:

- 1 tube crescent rolls
- 8 Oreos

Directions:

1. Wrap the Oreos in the crescent roll dough, trim off any excess
2. Spray the air fryer with cooking spray
3. Place Oreos in the air fryer and cook at 175°C for 6 minutes

Cinnamon-maple Pineapple Kebabs

Servings: 2
Cooking Time:xx

Ingredients:

- 4 x pineapple strips, roughly 2 x 2 cm/¾ x ¾ in. by length of pineapple
- 1 teaspoon maple syrup
- ½ teaspoon vanilla extract
- ¼ teaspoon ground cinnamon
- Greek or plant-based yogurt and grated lime zest, to serve

Directions:

1. Line the air-fryer with an air-fryer liner or a piece of pierced parchment paper. Preheat the air-fryer to 180°C/350°F.
2. Stick small metal skewers through the pineapple lengthways. Mix the maple syrup and vanilla extract together, then drizzle over the pineapple and sprinkle over the cinnamon.
3. Add the skewers to the preheated lined air-fryer and air-fry for 15 minutes, turning once. If there is any maple-vanilla mixture left after the initial drizzle, then drizzle this over the pineapple during cooking too. Serve with yogurt and lime zest.

Baked Nectarines

Servings: 4
Cooking Time:xx

Ingredients:

- 2 teaspoons maple syrup
- 1 teaspoon vanilla extract
- 1 teaspoon ground cinnamon
- 4 nectarines, halved and stones/pits removed
- chopped nuts, yogurt and runny honey, to serve (optional)

Directions:

1. Preheat the air-fryer to 180°C/350° F.
2. Mix the maple syrup, vanilla extract and cinnamon in a ramekin or shake in a jar to combine. Lay the nectarine halves on an air-fryer liner or piece of pierced parchment paper. Drizzle over the maple syrup mix.
3. Place in the preheated air-fryer and air-fry for 9–11 minutes, until soft when pricked with a fork. Serve scattered with chopped nuts and with a generous dollop of yogurt. Drizzle over some honey if you wish.

Brazilian Pineapple

Servings: 2
Cooking Time:xx

Ingredients:

- 1 small pineapple, cut into spears
- 100g brown sugar
- 2 tsp cinnamon
- 3 tbsp melted butter

Directions:

1. Mix the brown sugar and cinnamon together in a small bowl
2. Brush the pineapple with melted butter
3. Sprinkle with the sugar and cinnamon
4. Heat the air fryer to 200°C
5. Cook the pineapple for about 10 minutes

Peach Pies(2)

Servings: 8
Cooking Time:xx

Ingredients:

- 2 peaches, peeled and chopped
- 1 tbsp lemon juice
- 3 tbsp sugar
- 1 tsp vanilla extract
- ¼ tsp salt
- 1 tsp cornstarch
- 1 pack ready made pastry
- Cooking spray

Directions:

1. Mix together peaches, lemon juice, sugar and vanilla in a bowl. Stand for 15 minutes
2. Drain the peaches keeping 1 tbsp of the liquid, mix cornstarch into the peaches
3. Cut the pastry into 8 circles, fill with the peach mix
4. Brush the edges of the pastry with water and fold over to form half moons, crimp the edges to seal
5. Coat with cooking spray
6. Add to the air fryer and cook at 170°C for 12 minutes until golden brown

Chonut Holes

Servings: 12
Cooking Time:xx

Ingredients:

- 225g flour
- 75g sugar
- 1 tsp baking powder
- ¼ tsp cinnamon
- 2 tbsp sugar
- ½ tsp salt
- 2 tbsp aquafaba
- 1 tbsp melted coconut oil
- 75ml soy milk
- 2 tsp cinnamon

Directions:

1. In a bowl mix the flour, ¼ cup sugar, baking powder, ¼ tsp cinnamon and salt
2. Add the aquafaba, coconut oil and soy milk mix well
3. In another bowl mix 2 tsp cinnamon and 2 tbsp sugar
4. Line the air fryer with parchment paper
5. Divide the dough into 12 pieces and dredge with the cinnamon sugar mix
6. Place in the air fryer at 185°C and cook for 6-8 minutes, don‘t shake them

Milk And White Chocolate Chip Air Fryer Donuts With Frosting

Servings:4
Cooking Time:10 Minutes

Ingredients:

- For the donuts:
- 200 ml milk (any kind)
- 50 g / 3.5 oz brown sugar
- 50 g / 3.5 oz granulated sugar
- 1 tbsp active dry yeast
- 2 tbsp olive oil
- 4 tbsp butter, melted
- 1 egg, beaten
- 1 tsp vanilla extract
- 400 g / 14 oz plain flour
- 4 tbsp cocoa powder
- 100 g / 3.5 oz milk chocolate chips
- For the frosting:
- 5 tbsp powdered sugar
- 2 tbsp cocoa powder
- 100 ml heavy cream
- 50 g / 1.8 oz white chocolate chips, melted

Directions:

1. To make the donuts, whisk together the milk, brown and granulated sugars, and active dry yeast in a bowl. Set aside for a few minutes while the yeast starts to get foamy.
2. Stir the melted butter, beaten egg, and vanilla extract into the bowl. Mix well until all of the ingredients are combined.
3. Fold in the plain flour and cocoa powder until a smooth mixture forms.
4. Lightly flour a clean kitchen top surface and roll the dough out. Gently knead the dough for 2-3 minutes until it becomes soft and slightly tacky.
5. Transfer the dough into a large mixing bowl and cover it with a clean tea towel or some tinfoil. Leave the dough to rise for around one hour in a warm place.
6. Remove the tea towel or tinfoil from the bowl and roll it out on a floured surface once again. Use a rolling pin to roll the dough into a one-inch thick circle.
7. Use a round cookie cutter to create circular donuts and place each one into a lined air fryer basket.
8. Once all of the donuts have been placed into the air fryer, turn the machine onto 150 °C / 300 °F and close the lid.
9. Cook the donuts for 8-10 minutes until they are slightly golden and crispy on the outside.
10. While the donuts are cooking in the air fryer, make the frosting by combining the powdered sugar, cocoa powder, heavy cream, and melted white chocolate chips in a bowl. Mix well until a smooth, sticky mixture forms.
11. When the donuts are cooked, remove them from the air fryer and set aside to cool for 5-10 minutes. Once cooled, evenly spread some frosting on the top layer of each one. Place in the fridge to set for at least one hour.
12. Enjoy the donuts hot or cold.

Key Lime Cupcakes

Servings: 6
Cooking Time:xx

Ingredients:

- 250g Greek yogurt
- 200g soft cheese
- 2 eggs
- Juice and rind of 2 limes
- 1 egg yolk
- ¼ cup caster sugar
- 1 tsp vanilla essence

Directions:

1. Mix the Greek yogurt and soft cheese together until smooth
2. Add the eggs and mix, add the lime juice, rind, vanilla and caster sugar and mix well
3. Fill 6 cupcake cases with the mix and place the rest to one side
4. Place in the air fryer and cook at 160°C for 10 minutes then another 10 minutes at 180°C
5. Place the remaining mix into a piping bag, once the cupcakes have cooled pipe on the top and place in the fridge to set

Lemon Buns

Servings: 12
Cooking Time:xx

Ingredients:

- 100g butter
- 100g caster sugar
- 2 eggs
- 100g self raising flour
- ½ tsp vanilla essence
- 1 tsp cherries
- 50g butter
- 100g icing sugar
- ½ small lemon rind and juice

Directions:

1. Preheat the air fryer to 170°C
2. Cream the 100g butter, sugar and vanilla together until light and fluffy
3. Beat in the eggs one at a time adding a little flour with each
4. Fold in the remaining flour
5. Half fill bun cases with the mix, place in the air fryer and cook for 8 minutes
6. Cream 50g butter then mix in the icing sugar, stir in the lemon
7. Slice the top off each bun and create a butterfly shape using the icing to hold together. Add a 1/3 cherry to each one

Chocolate Orange Fondant

Servings: 4
Cooking Time:xx

Ingredients:

- 2 tbsp self raising flour
- 4 tbsp caster sugar
- 115g dark chocolate
- 115g butter
- 1 medium orange rind and juice
- 2 eggs

Directions:

1. Preheat the air fryer to 180°C and grease 4 ramekins
2. Place the chocolate and butter in a glass dish and melt over a pan of hot water, stir until the texture is creamy
3. Beat the eggs and sugar together until pale and fluffy
4. Add the orange and egg mix to the chocolate and mix
5. Stir in the flour until fully mixed together
6. Put the mix into the ramekins, place in the air fryer and cook for 12 minutes. Leave to stand for 2 minutes before serving

Chocolate Eclairs

Servings: 9
Cooking Time:xx

Ingredients:

- 100g plain flour
- 50g butter
- 3 eggs
- 150ml water
- 25g butter
- 1 tsp vanilla extract
- 1 tsp icing sugar
- 150ml whipped cream
- 50g milk chocolate
- 1 tbsp whipped cream

Directions:

1. Preheat the air fryer to 180°C
2. Add 50g of butter to a pan along with the water and melt over a medium heat
3. Remove from the heat and stir in the flour. Return to the heat until mix form a single ball of dough
4. Allow to cool, once cool beat in the eggs until you have a smooth dough
5. Make into eclair shapes, cook in the air fryer at 180°C for 10 minutes and then 160°C for 8 minutes
6. Mix the vanilla, icing sugar and 150ml of whipping cream until nice and thick
7. Once cool fill each eclair with the cream mix
8. Place the chocolate, 1 tbsp whipped cream and 25g of butter in a glass bowl and melt over a pan of boiling water. Top the eclairs

Banana Maple Flapjack

Servings:9
Cooking Time:xx
Ingredients:

- 100 g/7 tablespoons butter (or plant-based spread if you wish)
- 75 g/5 tablespoons maple syrup
- 2 ripe bananas, mashed well with the back of a fork
- 1 teaspoon vanilla extract
- 240 g/2½ cups rolled oats/quick-cooking oats

Directions:

1. Gently heat the butter and maple syrup in a medium saucepan over a low heat until melted. Stir in the mashed banana, vanilla and oats and combine all ingredients. Pour the flapjack mixture into a 15 x 15-cm/6 x 6-in. baking pan and cover with foil.
2. Preheat the air-fryer to 200°C/400°F.
3. Add the baking pan to the preheated air-fryer and air-fry for 12 minutes, then remove the foil and cook for a further 4 minutes to brown the top. Leave to cool before cutting into 9 squares.

Lemon Pies

Servings: 6
Cooking Time:xx
Ingredients:

- 1 pack of pastry
- 1 egg beaten
- 200g lemon curd
- 225g powdered sugar
- ½ lemon

Directions:

1. Preheat the air fryer to 180°C
2. Cut out 6 circles from the pastry using a cookie cutter
3. Add 1 tbsp of lemon curd to each circle, brush the edges with egg and fold over
4. Press around the edges of the dough with a fork to seal
5. Brush the pies with the egg and cook in the air fryer for 10 minutes
6. Mix the lemon juice with the powdered sugar to make the icing and drizzle on the cooked pies

Strawberry Danish

Servings: 2
Cooking Time:xx
Ingredients:

- 1 tube crescent roll dough
- 200g cream cheese
- 25g strawberry jam
- 50g diced strawberries
- 225g powdered sugar
- 2-3 tbsp cream

Directions:

1. Roll out the dough
2. Spread the cream cheese over the dough, cover in jam
3. Sprinkle with strawberries
4. Roll the dough up from the short side and pinch to seal
5. Line the air fryer with parchment paper and spray with cooking spray
6. Place the dough in the air fryer and cook at 175°C for 20 minutes
7. Mix the cream with the powdered sugar and drizzle on top once cooked

Chocolate Soufflé

Servings: 2
Cooking Time:xx

Ingredients:

- 150g semi sweet chocolate, chopped
- ¼ cup butter
- 2 eggs, separated
- 3 tbsp sugar
- ½ tsp vanilla extract
- 2 tbsp flour
- Icing sugar
- Whipped cream to serve

Directions:

1. Butter and sugar 2 small ramekins
2. Melt the chocolate and butter together
3. In another bowl beat the egg yolks, add the sugar and vanilla beat well
4. Drizzle in the chocolate mix well, add the flour and mix well
5. Preheat the air fryer to 165°C
6. Whisk the egg whites to soft peaks, gently fold into the chocolate mix a little at a time
7. Add the mix to ramekins and place in the air fryer. Cook for about 14 minutes
8. Dust with icing sugar, serve with whipped cream

Cinnamon Biscuit Bites

Servings: 16
Cooking Time:xx

Ingredients:

- 200g flour
- 200g wholewheat flour
- 2 tbsp sugar
- 1 tsp baking powder
- ¼ tsp cinnamon
- ¼ tsp salt
- 4 tbsp butter
- 50ml milk
- Cooking spray
- 300g icing sugar
- 3 tbsp water

Directions:

1. Mix together flour, salt, sugar baking powder and cinnamon in a bowl
2. Add butter and mix until well combined
3. Add milk and form a dough, place dough on a floured surface and knead until smooth
4. Cut into 16 equal pieces and form cach piecc into a ball
5. Place in the air fryer and cook at 180°C for about 12 minutes
6. Mix together icing sugar and water and coat to serve

Apple Chips With Yogurt Dip

Servings: 4
Cooking Time:xx
Ingredients:

- 1 apple
- 1 tsp cinnamon
- 2 tsp oil
- Cooking spray
- 25g greek yogurt
- 1 tbsp almond butter
- 1 tsp honey

Directions:

1. Thinly slice the apple, place in a bowl and coat with cinnamon and oil
2. Coat the air fryer with cooking spray and add the apple slices
3. Cook the slices for 12 minutes at 180°C
4. Mix the butter, honey and yogurt together and serve with the apple slices as a dip

Chocolate Souffle

Servings:2
Cooking Time:15 Minutes
Ingredients:

- 2 eggs
- 4 tbsp brown sugar
- 1 tsp vanilla extract
- 4 tbsp butter, melted
- 4 tbsp milk chocolate chips
- 4 tbsp flour

Directions:

1. Preheat the air fryer to 180 °C / 350 °F. Remove the mesh basket from the machine and line it with parchment paper.
2. Separate the egg whites from the egg yolks and place them in two separate bowls.
3. Beat the yolks together with the brown sugar, vanilla extract, melted butter, milk chocolate chips, and flour in a bowl. It should form a smooth, consistent mixture.
4. Whisk the egg whites until they form stiff peaks. In batches, fold the egg whites into the chocolate mixture.
5. Divide the batter evenly between two souffle dishes and place them in the lined air fryer basket.
6. Cook the souffle dishes for 15 minutes until hot and set.

Spiced Apples

Servings: 4
Cooking Time:xx
Ingredients:

- 4 apples, sliced
- 2 tbsp ghee
- 2 tbsp sugar
- 1 tsp apple pie spice

Directions:

1. Place apples in a bowl, add the ghee and sprinkle with sugar and apple pie spice
2. Place in a tin that will fit the air fryer
3. Heat the air fryer to 175°C
4. Put the tin in the air fryer and cook for 10 minutes until tender

Peach Pies(1)

Servings: 8
Cooking Time:xx

Ingredients:

- 2 peaches, peeled and chopped
- 1 tbsp lemon juice
- 3 tbsp sugar
- 1 tsp vanilla extract
- ¼ tsp salt
- 1 tsp cornstarch
- 1 pack of shortcrust pastry

Directions:

1. Stir together peaches, lemon juice, sugar, vanilla and salt allow to stand for 15 minutes
2. Drain the peaches keeping 1 tbsp of the juice
3. Mix the liquid with the cornstarch and mix into the peaches
4. Cut out 8 4 inch circles from the pastry. Add 1 tbsp of peach mix to each piece of pastry
5. Fold the dough over to create half moons, crimp the edges with a fork to seal. Spray with cooking spray
6. Place in the air fryer and cook at 180°C for 12-14 minutes

Breakfast Muffins

Servings:4
Cooking Time:xx

Ingredients:

- 1 eating apple, cored and grated
- 40 g/2 heaped tablespoons maple syrup
- 40 ml/3 tablespoons oil (avocado, olive or coconut), plus extra for greasing
- 1 egg
- 40 ml/3 tablespoons milk (plant-based if you wish)
- 90 g/scant ¾ cup brown rice flour
- 50 g/½ cup ground almonds
- ¾ teaspoon ground cinnamon
- ⅛ teaspoon ground cloves
- ¼ teaspoon salt
- 1 teaspoon baking powder
- Greek or plant-based yogurt and fresh fruit, to serve

Directions:

1. In a bowl mix the grated apple, maple syrup, oil, egg and milk. In another bowl mix the rice flour, ground almonds, cinnamon, cloves, salt and baking powder. Combine the wet ingredients with the dry, mixing until there are no visible patches of the flour mixture left. Grease 4 ramekins and divide the batter equally between them.
2. Preheat the air-fryer to 160°C/325°F.
3. Add the ramekins to the preheated air-fryer and air-fry for 12 minutes. Check the muffins are cooked by inserting a cocktail stick/toothpick into the middle of one of the muffins. If it comes out clean, the muffins are ready; if not, cook for a further couple of minutes.
4. Allow to cool in the ramekins, then remove and serve with your choice of yogurt and fresh fruit.

Pistachio Brownies

Servings: 4
Cooking Time:xx

Ingredients:

- 75ml milk
- ½ tsp vanilla extract
- 25g salt
- 25g pecans
- 75g flour
- 75g sugar
- 25g cocoa powder
- 1 tbsp ground flax seeds

Directions:

1. Mix all of the dry ingredients together, in another bowl mix the wet ingredients
2. Add all the ingredients together and mix well
3. Preheat the air fryer to 175°C
4. Line a 5 inch cake tin with parchment paper
5. Pour the brownie mix into the cake tin and cook in the air fryer for about 20 minutes

Banana Bread

Servings: 8
Cooking Time:xx

Ingredients:

- 200g flour
- 1 tsp cinnamon
- ½ tsp salt
- ¼ tsp baking soda
- 2 ripe banana mashed
- 2 large eggs
- 75g sugar
- 25g plain yogurt
- 2 tbsp oil
- 1 tsp vanilla extract
- 2 tbsp chopped walnuts
- Cooking spray

Directions:

1. Line a 6 inch cake tin with parchment paper and coat with cooking spray
2. Whisk together flour, cinnamon, salt and baking soda set aside
3. In another bowl mix together remaining ingredients, add the flour mix and combine well
4. Pour batter into the cake tin and place in the air fryer
5. Cook at 155°C for 35 minutes turning halfway through

Chocolate Cake

Servings: 2
Cooking Time:xx
Ingredients:

- 3 eggs
- 75ml sour cream
- 225g flour
- 150g sugar
- 2 tsp vanilla extract
- 25g cocoa powder
- 1 tsp baking powder
- ½ tsp baking soda

Directions:

1. Preheat the air fryer to 160°C
2. Mix all the ingredients together in a bowl
3. Pour into a greased baking tin
4. Place into the air fryer and cook for 25 minutes
5. Allow to cool and ice with chocolate frosting

Chocolate Shortbread Balls

Servings: 9
Cooking Time:13 Minutes
Ingredients:

- 175g butter
- 75g caster sugar
- 250g plain flour
- 2 tsp vanilla essence
- 9 chocolate chunks
- 2 tbsp cocoa powder

Directions:

1. Preheat the air fryer to 180°C
2. Add the flour, sugar and cocoa to a bowl and mix well
3. Rub in the butter and vanilla then knead into a smooth dough
4. Divide the mix into 9, place a chunk of chocolate in each piece and form into balls covering the chocolate
5. Place the balls in the air fryer and cook at 180°C for 8 mins then a further 6 mins at 160°C

Sugar Dough Dippers

Servings: 12
Cooking Time:xx
Ingredients:

- 300g bread dough
- 75g melted butter
- 100g sugar
- 200ml double cream
- 200g semi sweet chocolate
- 2 tbsp amaretto

Directions:

1. Roll the dough into 2 15inch logs, cut each one into 20 slices. Cut each slice in half and twist together 2-3 times. Brush with melted butter and sprinkle with sugar
2. Preheat the air fryer to 150°C
3. Place dough in the air fryer and cook for 5 minutes, turnover and cook for a further 3 minutes
4. Place the cream in a pan and bring to simmer over a medium heat, place the chocolate chips in a bowl and pour over the cream
5. Mix until the chocolate is melted then stir in the amaretto
6. Serve the dough dippers with the chocolate dip

Fruit Scones

Servings: 4
Cooking Time:xx

Ingredients:

- 225g self raising flour
- 50g butter
- 50g sultanas
- 25g caster sugar
- 1 egg
- A little milk

Directions:

1. Place the flour in a bowl and rub in the butter, add the sultanas and mix
2. Stir in the caster sugar
3. Add the egg and mix well
4. Add a little bit of milk at a time to form a dough
5. Shape the dough into scones
6. Place in the air fryer and bake at 180°C for 8 minutes

Grilled Ginger & Coconut Pineapple Rings

Servings: 4
Cooking Time:xx

Ingredients:

- 1 medium pineapple
- coconut oil, melted
- 1½ teaspoons coconut sugar
- ½ teaspoon ground ginger
- coconut or vanilla yogurt, to serve

Directions:

1. Preheat the air-fryer to 180°C/350°F.
2. Peel and core the pineapple, then slice into 4 thick rings.
3. Mix together the melted coconut oil with the sugar and ginger in a small bowl. Using a pastry brush, paint this mixture all over the pineapple rings, including the sides of the rings.
4. Add the rings to the preheated air-fryer and air-fry for 20 minutes. Check after 18 minutes as pineapple sizes vary and your rings may be perfectly cooked already. You'll know they are ready when they're golden in colour and a fork can easily be inserted with very little resistance
5. Serve warm with a generous spoonful of yogurt.

RECIPES INDEX

A

Air Fried Maple Chicken Thighs 72

Air Fried Scallops 61

Air Fryer Cheese Sandwich 43

Air Fryer Chicken Thigh Schnitzel 78

Air Fryer Sesame Chicken Thighs 80

Air Fryer Tuna 63

Air-fried Artichoke Hearts 32

Apple Chips With Yogurt Dip 100

Apple Crumble 92

Arancini 39

Artichoke Pasta 41

Asian Meatballs 58

Aubergine Dip 37

Aubergine Parmigiana 31

B

Baked Nectarines 93

Baked Potato 36

Banana Bread 102

Banana Maple Flapjack 98

Bbq Chicken Tenders 79

Beef And Cheese Empanadas 52

Beef Bulgogi Burgers 48

Beef Nacho Pinwheels 58

Beef Satay 47

Beef Stirfry 50

Beef Stroganoff 59

Beef Stuffed Peppers 52

Beetroot Crisps 24

Blanket Breakfast Eggs 17

Blueberry Bread 12

Bocconcini Balls 18

Brazilian Pineapple 93

Breakfast Eggs & Spinach 17

Breakfast Muffins 101

Breakfast Sausage Burgers 15

Broccoli Cheese 39

Butter Steak & Asparagus 53

Butternut Squash 87

Butternut Squash Falafel 43

C

Butternut Squash Fries 86

Cajun Prawn Skewers 63

Cajun Shrimp Boil 67

Cauliflower With Hot Sauce And Blue Cheese Sauce 85

Celery Root Fries 86

Char Siu Buffalo 57

Cheese & Ham Sliders 59

Cheese Scones 13

Cheese Wontons 23

Cheesy Beef Enchiladas 55

Cheesy Sausage Breakfast Pockets 18

Chicken And Cheese Chimichangas 76

Chicken And Wheat Stir Fry 69

Chicken Fajitas 76

Chicken Fried Rice 75

Chicken Jalfrezi 78

Chicken Milanese 77

Chicken Tikka 73

Chinese Chilli Beef 58

Chocolate Cake 103

Chocolate Eclairs 97

Chocolate Orange Fondant 97

Chocolate Orange Muffins 90

Chocolate Shortbread Balls 103
Chocolate Souffle 100
Chocolate Soufflé 99
Chonut Holes 94
Cinnamon Biscuit Bites 99
Cinnamon-maple Pineapple Kebabs 93
Coconut Shrimp 62
Cod Nuggets 68
Copycat Burger 57
Corn On The Cob 89
Cornflake Chicken Nuggets 74
Courgette Gratin 89
Crispy Chili Sausages 56
Crispy Cinnamon French Toast 88
Crispy Cornish Hen 80
Crispy Nacho Prawns 66
Crispy Potato Peels 39
Crispy Sweet & Spicy Cauliflower 82
Crunchy Chicken Tenders 72
Crunchy Fish 67

E

Easy Cheesy Scrambled Eggs 12
Egg & Bacon Breakfast Cups 16
Egg Fried Rice 83
European Pancakes 18

F

Falafel Burgers 38
Fish In Foil 61
Fish Sticks With Tartar Sauce Batter 65
Focaccia Bread 25
French Toast Slices 16
Fried Oreos 92
Fruit Scones 104

G

Garlic And Parsley Potatoes 82
Garlic Parmesan Fried Chicken Wings 70
Garlic Tilapia 65
Garlic-parsley Prawns 68
Gluten Free Honey And Garlic Shrimp 66
Gnocchi Caprese 33
Goat's Cheese Tartlets 35
Grain-free Chicken Katsu 71
Grilled Ginger & Coconut Pineapple Rings 104

H

Hamburgers 51
Hamburgers With Feta 51
Hard Boiled Eggs Air Fryer Style 15
Hasselback New Potatoes 89
Hawaiian Chicken 70
Healthy Stuffed Peppers 19
Homemade Crispy Pepperoni Pizza 54
Homemade Croquettes 84

I

Italian Rice Balls 24

J

Jalapeño Pockets 28
Jalapeño Poppers 27
Jamaican Jerk Pork 46
Japanese Pork Chops 45

K

Key Lime Cupcakes 96
Korean Chicken Wings 22

L

Lemon Buns 96
Lemon Pies 98
Lentil Balls With Zingy Rice 32
Lentil Burgers 36
Loaded Hash Browns 13
Lumpia 26

M

Maine Seafood 65

Mexican Rice 84

Milk And White Chocolate Chip Air Fryer Donuts With Frosting 95

Mini Aubergine Parmesan Pizza 27

Mini Calzones 30

Mini Egg Buns 90

Miso Mushrooms On Sourdough Toast 40

Monte Cristo Breakfast Sandwich 19

Morning Sausage Wraps 20

Mustard Pork Tenderloin 55

N

Nashville Chicken 75

O

Old Fashioned Steak 47

Onion Pakoda 21

Oozing Baked Eggs 19

Orange Chicken 79

Orange Tofu 88

Orange Zingy Cauliflower 40

P

Pao De Queijo 28

Peach Pies(1) 101

Peach Pies(2) 94

Peppers With Aioli Dip 26

Peppery Lemon Shrimp 69

Pesto Salmon 64

Pistachio Brownies 102

Pizza Chicken Nuggets 74

Plantain Fries 12

Polenta Fries 14

Popcorn Tofu 25

Pork Chops With Raspberry And Balsamic 50

Pork Taquitos 56

Pork With Chinese 5 Spice 51

Potato & Chorizo Frittata 15

Potato Wedges 82

Potato Wedges With Rosemary 87

Pulled Pork, Bacon, And Cheese Sliders 49

Q

Quick Chicken Nuggets 77

R

Radish Hash Browns 44

Rainbow Vegetables 43

Ranch Style Fish Fillets 67

Raspberry Breakfast Pockets 14

Ricotta Stuffed Aubergine 81

Roast Cauliflower & Broccoli 34

Roasted Cauliflower 36

Roasted Garlic 31

S

Saganaki 41

Salmon Patties 60

Salt & Pepper Calamari 66

Salt And Pepper Belly Pork 46

Salt And Vinegar Chickpeas 29

Satay Tofu Skewers 30

Sausage Gnocchi One Pot 54

Scotch Eggs 29

Shishito Peppers 83

Shortbread Cookies 91

Spanakopita Bites 38

Spiced Apples 100

Spicy Egg Rolls 21

Spicy Green Beans 83

Spinach And Egg Air Fryer Breakfast Muffins 42

Spring Ratatouille 35

Steak And Mushrooms 49

Steak Dinner 45
Steak Popcorn Bites 56
Sticky Asian Beef 46
Sticky Tofu With Cauliflower Rice 37
Store-cupboard Fishcakes 68
Strawberry Danish 98
Strawberry Lemonade Pop Tarts 91
Sugar Dough Dippers 103
Swede Fries 20
Sweet And Sticky Parsnips And Carrots 81
Sweet Potato Crisps 23
Sweet Potato Fries 17
Sweet Potato Taquitos 34
Sweet Potato Tots 86

T

Tahini Beef Bites 53
Tempura Veggies 44
Thai Bites 23
Thai Fish Cakes 62
Thai Fried Bananas 92
Thai Salmon Patties 61
Thai Turkey Burgers 73
Thai-style Tuna Fishcakes 60
Tomato And Herb Tofu 42
Tortellini Bites 22
Tostones 29
Traditional Empanadas 48
Traditional Fish And Chips 64

V

Veggie Bakes 41
Veggie Lasagne 33

W

Waffle Fries 27
Whole Chicken 79
Whole Wheat Pizza 35

Z

Zingy Brussels Sprouts 87
Zingy Roasted Carrots 85

Printed in Great Britain
by Amazon

41598619R00064